Me May Mary

Mary Cameron Kilgour

To Peter - fellow Foreign
Service Officer.

Mary Cameron Kilgour

Child Welfare League of America
WASHINGTON, DC

The Child Welfare League of America is the nation's oldest and largest membership-based child welfare organization. We are committed to engaging people everywhere in promoting the well-being of children, youth, and their families, and protecting every child from harm.

CHILD WELFARE LEAGUE OF AMERICA, INC.
Headquarters
440 First Street, NW, Third Floor, Washington, DC 20001-2085
E-mail: books@cwla.org

CURRENT PRINTING (last digit)
10 9 8 7 6 5 4 3 2 1

Cover and text design by Amy Alick
Edited by Julie Gwin
Printed in the United States of America

ISBN-13: 978-1-58760-018-0
ISBN-10: 1-58760-018-8

Library of Congress Cataloging-in-Publication Data

Kilgour, Mary Cameron.
Me May Mary / Mary Cameron Kilgour.
    p. cm.
ISBN 1-58760-018-8 (alk. paper)
1. Kilgour, Mary Cameron--Childhood and youth. 2. Abused children--United States--Biography. 3. Adult child abuse victims--United States--Biography. 4. Children of alcoholics--United States--Biography. I. Title.
HV6626.52.K555 2005
362.76'092--dc22

2004002352

Contents

For Jack
and
For my guardian ad litem children:
H, G, M, C, T, L, L, B,
and
For those still to come

ACKNOWLEDGMENTS

Many people have helped turn my story into a book. I greatly appreciate the contributions of the editorial staff at the Child Welfare League of America (CWLA), not only for publishing my memoir, but also for everything CWLA does to advocate for children throughout our country. For the same reason, I respect and support as a volunteer the admirable work of guardian ad litem and court-appointed special advocate programs. Without such organizations, especially the guardian ad litem program in Gainesville, Florida, I would not have had the opportunity to help today's abused and neglected children and probably would never have written this memoir.

Many friends have read and improved the manuscript that became *Me May Mary*. Taking the easy way out, I acknowledge in alphabetical order their valuable comments on the draft and their encouragement at crucial times: Carah Lynne Billups, Linda Cantrell, Anna DeFronzo, Sandy Del Prado, Lawrence Dorr, Joyce Fox, Betty Jennings, Jack and Jan Kilgour, Mag McGauley, Marilyn Maple, Shelley Fraser Mickle, Anita Thebeault, and Kate Wilkinson. Those I made cry get a special thanks.

The only characters in this book who are undisguised are my brother, my parents, and myself. To respect the privacy of all others, they have been turned into composites or altered so that only they will be able to identify themselves. This story is true, although I had to make some alterations in the timeline and events in the interest of coherence. Only I have responsibility for whatever errors or misinterpretations remain.

Mary Cameron Kilgour
Gainesville, Florida

PART 1

Downward

CHAPTER 1

Sneaking Out

"Me, where are you? Me? Answer me!" She swayed into the kitchen in slow motion and grabbed ahold of the sink to steady herself. Her faded blue bathrobe was open and showed part of a breast that sagged to her stomach like a balloon almost out of air. Her Scottish pronunciation of my nickname, May, was loud enough for the neighbors to hear. Some of them had already asked about the crazy woman who sometimes called out to herself from her front window.

At the age of eleven, back in 1952, I knew I didn't want to be like my mother, with her drinking and fighting and Scottish ways. But I lived each day as it came. Right then I was trying to get out of the house to join my friends for a rafting trip on the Hog River. I thought I could get away before she woke up to start an argument, a barrage of insults. No such luck.

"Where do you think you're going dressed like that?" She fixed me with a glare. Her voice was hoarse.

I looked down at my two-piece bathing suit under a pair of blue shorts and a red unbuttoned blouse. What was wrong? "It's Saturday. I told you I was going rafting. Remember I said we found a raft on the Hog River and were going to float it through the city?"

"No you're not. You look like a tramp."

"Ma," I groaned. "All my friends are going."

"Your brother is already down at your father's work helping him. There's plenty for you to do around here since you're not helping there."

I decided not to argue the point that I wasn't down helping Daddy because she had decided herself not to go. "Like what?"

"You can start by emptying the trash. Then wash out those clothes soaking in the tub."

My mother smelled of whiskey. She made her way toward her black leather and chrome chair rescued long ago from the ladies' room at Dad's work. I stepped back, bracing myself, because Mom taking an interest in cleaning the apartment was one of the signs that she was in a bad mood. The apartment's mess was proof that this particular interest didn't come up very often, but I remembered the previous Christmas, the glass she threw at me because I wasn't washing them fast enough. It didn't break, but it raised a bruise at the corner of my eyebrow that everyone could see and wonder about, something I had to lie about, to hide.

I edged around the other side of the table and reached for the paper bag inside the metal trashcan. "Okay. I'll get the one in the bathroom too."

I went to the bathroom and emptied the waste paper basket into the larger bag. I looked at myself in the mirror hanging behind the bathroom door. A straight crack in the mirror from the top left to the bottom right, with a quarter inch gap between the two halves, split me in two. Sometimes that's how I felt. But did I look like a tramp? It was true my shorts were tight, but my other, newer pair was soaking in the laundry tub. What exactly did a tramp look like? Was Mom talking about the women in tight dresses and puffed-up hair at the cocktail lounge next to the Lenox Theatre? Or was she talking about the bums on the streets downtown? My thin figure was that of a tomboy, someone good at sports. I didn't think I looked anything like the women Dad called floozies. My face was ordinary, not pretty, but not ugly either. A ponytail corralled my straight dirty-blonde hair in an okay way. My blouse was faded and also a little tight. But all in all I thought I looked like most of the other kids my age. So today was one of those days when I needed to stay as far away from Mom as I could. Besides, I needed to get to the Hog River. My friends were waiting.

With my sneaker I squashed the trash down, then folded over the top of the bag and carried it through the kitchen without speaking to Mom, who sat in her chair smoking and reading the *Hartford Courant*. In the living room, where my older brother, Jacky, and I slept, I picked up a rolled towel from my couch bed. We lived in one of those apartments laid out in a straight line, a railroad flat, I think they were called: living room then kitchen then small hallway and bath then bedroom. The living room and the hallway each had a door out to a common corridor we shared with three other apartments. The other apartments in the building were nice. Ours was not. Part of the ceiling in the kitchen had fallen down, leaving exposed boards and chunks of dusty plaster, and the place hadn't been painted in my entire lifetime. The living room rug had gotten so old and stained, we had thrown it out and left the wood floor uncovered.

With the towel in one arm and the trash in the other, I opened the living room door quietly and hurried along the corridor to the back stairs and down to the graveled backyard shared by two apartment buildings. Opening the wooden door to the garbage shed caused rats to scurry toward the back, away from the light, away from me, an intruding giant. Watching each step to avoid the fat white maggots near the garbage bins and breathing through my mouth, I opened several barrels before finding one with room for the bag. I hated this shed that all twenty-four families living in the two buildings used. But it was my job to empty the trash.

From the garbage shed, I went to the weed-filled alley on the far side of the apartment building next to mine, in case Mom decided to look out the kitchen window into the driveway and shout something mean or embarrassing. Today she was in a mood to call me nasty names and order me back to the apartment, as if I were still a little kid. Forget about that. I'd catch up with my friends and worry later about the consequences of sneaking out.

At the end of the alley, I headed down Woodland Street toward Homestead Avenue and the house of my best friend, Joanie Dresser. I had lived on Woodland all my life, had even been born four blocks down at St. Francis Hospital. The scene was totally familiar: the tall elm trees and three-story apartment buildings like mine of yellow and red brick mixed in with older wooden houses, along with the Eagle Dye Works, which was a dry cleaning plant, and a small grocery store called Saul's. The Dutch Elm trees would all be dead by the time I was grown, turning the street harsh and poor, but in my childhood, they were majestic and beautiful. I wiped the sweat off my forehead with the back of my hand, thinking about the water and shade on the Hog River. It really was hot for early June in Hartford. School wasn't even out yet.

I saw Lenore Feeney coming down the street and waved.

"Hi Lenore." She was a year younger than I and in the fifth grade, a year behind me. Short and plump, but pretty, with rosy cheeks, she had Shirley Temple curls that I wished I had. "Where's Joanie?"

"I think she had to go someplace with her mother. No one else showed. Maybe they'll meet us there."

"Oh, okay. Let's take a shortcut through those yards." I pointed across the tree-shaded street, thinking about my mother's mood and not wanting to pass in front of my building. Deep inside me, I knew I loved her, but there was something wrong between us. She seemed sometimes to dislike me, to blame me for things that weren't my fault. She didn't do this as much with Jacky, although sometimes her fights with Dad got real ugly. I didn't want my friends to know any of this. I wanted to come from a normal, respectable family, like they did.

On the other side of the street, I had to slow my long-legged step to match Lenore's shorter one.

"What're you doing this summer?" she asked me.

"Going to camp for two weeks. You?"

"We're going to Lake Winnipesaukee for a month like we always do, to my grandmother's house."

"That should be nice." Lenore's family was normal as far as I knew. Her father was a teacher.

"Which camp?"

"Times Farm."

"Never heard of it. Is it Girl Scouts?"

"No. It's out in Andover, beyond Manchester." I didn't want to tell her that the afternoon newspaper, the *Hartford Times,* ran it, that it was for kids who couldn't afford regular camp.

"Sounds like more fun than being with my family for a whole month."

"Maybe. I enjoyed it last summer."

We came out on Albany Avenue and walked past the library, the Popular Market, a string of small stores, and a row of three-decker wooden houses painted long ago in shades of brown and gray. At the edge of the neighborhood we took a path from the busy avenue through fields overgrown with weeds and pink wildflowers. As the path entered the woods, two sweaty-looking boys who had been sitting on a rock got up. They seemed to be waiting for us.

"Lenore, do you know those boys?"

"No."

"Me neither."

The boys were dressed alike in khaki shorts and faded tee shirts, and their heads had been shaved practically bald.

"Hi," they said at the same time.

"Hi. Are there some kids from Northwest at the river?" I asked.

"Yeah. They're already swimming. C'mon."

That explained why the other kids hadn't met us on Woodland. Maybe we had missed them, with Lenore waiting for Joanie and me having to take out the garbage. I didn't have a watch, though I desperately wanted one. We followed the boys along the path into the woods bordering the river, which was narrow at this point. Even at the edge of the city the river was polluted, though not bad enough to scare us off, and it smelled only of humid air. The brown water was so dull it gave off little reflection of the overhanging green leaves, or of the soft blue sky.

I could hear splashing and shouting in the distance—welcoming, cooling sounds. For being so near the city, it was tranquil, like being out in the country. Traffic sounds gave way to the hum of insects and the chatter of squirrels. Yellow butterflies danced along the edges of the path. A spider web in the shade still held a few drops of dew.

The path ended in a small sunlit grassy clearing. Bushes and trees edged all sides. The river at this point was maybe fifty feet across. Two boys in the water horse-played with each other and a boy I knew from school, Jimmy Costa, sat on a raft, which was tied to a tree. He waved.

The two boys who had led us through the woods both took their shorts off and jumped into the water in their jockey underpants. That was surprising, swimming without bathing trunks in front of girls and not saying anything. I looked at Lenore and saw that she was surprised too.

CHAPTER 2

Betrayal at Hog River

Jimmy Costa swam across the river to our side and climbed out of the water. He was a handsome boy with big brown eyes and close-cropped black hair. I'd known him since Mrs. Lotty's kindergarten class. He wasn't too bright, but seemed nice enough and through all the years at Northwest Elementary we had been in the same large school crowd, although he lived on the outskirts of my neighborhood.

"Hey, Jimmy, didn't any other girls show up?" I tried to sound cool, to hide my unease.

"It's just you two. I don't know them either," he said, gesturing to the two boys. "They're from the orphanage." He waved his arm across the river where a cluster of brick buildings could be seen through the woods. It was a home for foster children. Most of the kids who lived there didn't stay long, and no one at school got to know them well. Those who did stay for a year or more seemed nice enough, but some of the short-timers got into trouble at school and stole from the other kids when they got the chance. They all seemed pretty poor.

Two boys who had been playing in the water climbed onto the shore.

"Hi. I'm Bobby," one of them said. "I've seen you in school. You're in Ms. Brown's class, aren't you?" He was husky and older than I, perhaps thirteen, though we were in the same grade.

I nodded. "Yeah. I'm May." His face was oddly blank, no smile, just words coming out. I couldn't read his expression.

Lenore told them her name and the other boy, flashing a smile, said his name was Kevin. He was cute, red haired and freckled. "Hey Lenore. Want to go for a swim?"

"What about rafting?"

"We can do that later. C'mon."

Lenore sat down to unlace her sneakers and take off her socks. She stood again to take off the orange blouse and white pedal pushers she had on over her bathing suit, folded everything neatly on her shoes with the towel and carefully placed it all under a tree. She had on a pretty blue two-piece bathing suit that looked new, at least compared to mine.

Kevin grabbed her hand and said, "Let's do it quick. The water's cold."

They jumped together into the slow-moving murky water shouting and splashing, then started swimming upstream. Lenore stopped long enough to call to me.

"Come on in, May. It's not too bad."

Bobby came up close to me. He too had his hair shaved off except for a small light brown patch on top. His eyes were small and the irises were light blue or gray. In the glare of the sun I could hardly distinguish them from the whites of his eyes. "You want to go swimming, May?"

"I guess so. Is the water really cold?"

"Yeah, it's real cold."

I didn't like the idea of Lenore and me being the only girls. Could we trust these boys? I had no strong reason not to, but still, I'd feel better if Joanie, Stella, and some of the other girls had come. I kicked off my sneakers and tossed them with my towel over near Lenore's. I looked at Bobby and for the first time he smiled. Reassured, I took off my shorts and blouse and put them on top of the pile. Two new boys came along the path wearing bathing suits. They didn't introduce themselves but said hi and stood on the riverbank as if debating whether to jump in. Again I felt uneasy, self-conscious, with a bunch of boys I didn't know watching me. What were they thinking? Lenore was already up the river, barely visible through the trees, her voice with Kevin's making sounds whose sense was lost in the distance.

I walked over to the bank of the river. Bobby and the two newcomers stood on the shore with me. The two in their underwear treaded water in the river and I felt them looking at me. I couldn't see Jimmy anywhere.

Everything seemed to be standing still. I felt a chill again and saw goose bumps on my arms, though the air was sticky hot.

Suddenly the two boys on the riverbank rushed toward me and each grabbed one of my arms. They pulled me backward toward the soft grass of the clearing. My stomach lurched.

"Hey, let go! What're you doing?"

Bobby was in front of me, coming closer, no longer smiling. "The water's too cold. Let's play around a little first," he said.

"Let me go!" My heart was pounding, my throat tightening as it did when I wolfed down peanuts too fast without a drink. "What's going on?"

"C'mon, May. Let's see what you've got."

I tried to pull my arms free but the boys held them tight. The air was so bright and still I had to force myself to focus. Bobby was sneering now. I could see beads of sweat above his lip. He pulled roughly at the halter of my bathing suit until it came loose, uncovering my chest with my little pointy-bump breasts showing.

"Stop it! Let me go!" I kicked at Bobby. Fear rushed through my body like floodwater. I kept kicking at him to keep him away.

"Hold her legs," he shouted. The two boys who had been swimming in their underpants climbed out of the water. Each grabbed one of my legs. I was still standing but I couldn't move. Their wet clinging underpants made them seem naked. I swung my arms as much as I could, forcing the boys to move back and forth with me. They tightened their grip. My arms hurt from their twisting. The sun beat down. My nose filled with the smell of sweat and squashed grass and I started to cry. I hated to cry in front of these boys, because it made me seem weak when I needed to be strong and brave, to fight back. But I couldn't help it.

Bobby grabbed at the bottom of my bathing suit and tried to pull it down over my hips. I jerked my body back and forth and sideways and squeezed my legs tightly together. His hands kept sliding off me. *I had to stay standing. I had to stay standing.* Sweat ran down his mean red face. I looked through the trees to the sky and screamed as loud as I could. My mouth felt like it was filling with sawdust.

"C'mon, you want this. That's why you came!"

"No! Get away from me!" Want this? Is he crazy? What girl would want this? I had read enough *True Confessions* and *True Crime* magazines

to see what was happening, what could happen. I twisted my head toward
the traffic on Albany Avenue. People must be walking there with their
wheeled carts, going to the First National supermarket, old people, hard
of hearing and feeble. "Help! Help!"

"Hold her tighter!"

"God damn you! Help! Help!" Why didn't anyone come? We were
only a couple of blocks from the street. Why was this happening? My
mother was going to kill me. *I told you so, I told you so. Tramp!* My screams
reached into the sky and the birds were quiet.

My swimsuit bottom was twisted around my knees. I was still standing, a small victory, but I was bare in front of all these boys. No one was
laughing.

I screamed and cried at the same time. I felt my face fix into a grimace
and my voice became a shriek. It seemed like forever. Tasting tears of dirt
and sweat, I could see Jimmy Costa standing off from the other boys in
the woods beyond the clearing, looking at the ground. Where had he
been? Hiding? What was he thinking? Why didn't he help me?

"Oh come on, leave her alone. She doesn't want it," said not Jimmy,
but a boy I didn't know who was in the water by the raft.

"Yeah. The hell with it." The one holding my right leg let it go and
made a running jump into the water. He started to drift downstream with
the current.

For a moment nothing else happened. I could hear the cars on the
avenue, the splash of water. Bobby shoved me hard at the chest, intending
to hurt me. But the pressure of the three boys still holding on kept me
from falling. Bobby turned his back on me and headed toward the river.
The other boys let go.

"Bastard!" I wished I were a boy his size so I could beat him up fair
and square with my fists, or even bigger so I could hold his head under the
water until he felt the same terror I had just felt. He dived into the water
and disappeared.

Was I safe now? I couldn't be sure. I pulled up my swimsuit quickly
and retied the top with hands shaking so badly I almost couldn't do it. I
put my clothes on over my bathing suit. My skin felt clammy and my arms
were red and sore. Everything about me was aching, inside and out. Jimmy
came up to me, already dressed. He looked so clean and untouched.

"You too, you ratfink!" I felt a tremendous rage, mixed with shame, load itself on top of the ache.

"Are you okay?"

What a dumb question. I wouldn't even answer him. I walked up the path the way we had come. I heard his footsteps following, scuffling through broken twigs and old leaves. Around a bend in the path, Lenore and Kevin sat on a fallen tree trunk. Lenore, still wet, was crying. She jumped up.

"Are you okay, May?

"No. Those dirty rotten rats. Are you?"

She nodded. "But he wouldn't let me out of the water and he kept trying to feel me up." She pointed at Kevin, still sitting on the log.

He stood up, looking scared. "I'll go get your clothes." He ran back down the path, returned with Lenore's things and held them out to her. She snatched them and we walked along the path away from him. Lenore put on her clothes as we walked, hopping and running to match my faster pace. I wanted to get out of those woods fast. Jimmy followed behind.

When we were well into the field of pink wildflowers, I turned to Jimmy. "You knew what was going to happen. Why didn't you warn us?"

"I didn't know for sure. They talked about it, but I didn't think they were serious." He ran his hand back and forth through his short curly hair as if trying to shake out something unpleasant.

Before we reached the street I scrubbed my face with my towel and fixed my ponytail. I dreaded what was going to happen next. If those boys bragged, it would spread all over the school. My reputation would be ruined.

"Jimmy, you better keep your mouth shut about this."

"Don't worry, I won't say anything."

"I won't either, May. My parents will kill me if they find out."

Now I had to go home and face my parents and Jacky. I couldn't tell them. Jacky would feel my shame and want to fight them all. Dad would blame me; I shouldn't have gone there; he would call me bad, grown-up names, words from Scotland that no one else I knew ever used, words he called Mom when he was on the nasty side of drunkenness, before he fell asleep sitting up in the kitchen. Mom would say the same thing and maybe take a swing at me. And she'd be angrier because of this morning, if she hadn't already gotten drunk and forgotten about it. My parents would not come to my rescue, I had learned that already. I would have to face the worst thing that had ever happened to me alone.

CHAPTER 3

Waiting for Camp

Sure enough, in school on Monday I could hear kids whispering, see them staring at me and nudging each other, then looking away if I caught their eye. I cringed inside and took to looking only at my desk or at the teacher. Over the next few days, word spread not just that my bathing suit had been pulled off but that the orphanage boys had raped me.

My girlfriends asked, "Is it true?"

"No, it's not true." But I wouldn't say more, even to my best friends, Joanie Dresser and Stella Pagano, the two who should have been there with me. If they had been there, maybe it wouldn't have happened. But I couldn't blame them for that, and I couldn't say anything to defend myself or explain it. I just wanted to pretend it didn't happen, like I already did with parts of my family life.

Joanie put her arm around my shoulder, whispering, "It's okay. Forget about it and everyone else will too." She said she was sorry about leaving me in the lurch and I could tell she was sincere.

Stella said that her parents wouldn't let her out, and then handed me a whole bag of pistachio nuts, like flowers to a hospital patient.

I avoided everyone else and fed my anger and shame with my thoughts. I hated Bobby and the other boys. Somehow I hated Jimmy even more for not warning me. I thought he was my friend. We had played spin the bottle in the attic of his house at his last birthday party and had kissed twice, nice kisses, soft and not too wet. We had laughed hilariously together when the volcano we built in fifth-grade science exploded, spewing ash and papier-mâché all over the teacher and us. Why hadn't he told me to stay away? Was it my fault? Was I a tramp? A bad girl? Would I become a floozy when I grew up?

In bits and pieces over the remaining days of school, the story changed, getting more accurate among my friends and worse to those who weren't my friends. I had been raped by all of the boys there. No, I had been stripped, not raped. My clothes had been pulled off and the boys had seen me naked. I had asked for it. It was my fault.

I said nothing, trying to blot it out. Ignore it, forget about it, I told myself. Yet a tension like ice about to crack seized my body. Bobby's sweaty face inches away popped into my mind without warning every day. I lived in fear of my parents and in shame of my brother, Jacky, finding out.

* * *

Sixth-grade graduation from Northwest meant most of all that the whispering and stares might stop. At least that was my hope. Most of my classmates would scatter until the fall, when maybe they would have forgotten about it. I yearned to go backwards to what I remembered as a carefree, tomboy existence. This summer I'd hang out with Joanie and Stella and maybe the neighborhood kids. I broke down and explained, in a very brief version, what happened to Sheila and Beth, who lived in the next apartment building, knowing they'd spread the word.

"It's not as bad as what I heard," Beth said. But Sheila added, "It still must've been awful. Weren't you afraid? I mean, to even go there?"

"I went there before and nothing happened. It was fun the first two times." Did Sheila, like Bobby, think I wanted it to happen? That I was a tramp, like my mother said?

I saw Lenore only once before school ended.

"I'm scared my parents are going to find out. So far they don't know." Her father was a teacher at the junior high school.

"Mine don't know either."

"I hope I never see that guy, Kevin, again. You know he said he'd drown me if I tried to escape."

"He did? Really drown you?"

"Yeah, and later he told me their plan was to rape both of us and throw us into the river."

Could it have come to that, raping, even trying to drown us both? That seemed pretty far out, beyond even these boys' capability. "Kevin seemed pretty scared himself afterward. Do you think he really meant it?"

Lenore shrugged. "Maybe not. He apologized, said he didn't believe Bobby would really do it. But it sure was scary."

"Yeah. I never want to go through that again. But maybe we were lucky." I didn't feel lucky. I felt torn, stained, more grown up than I was ready to be.

* * *

Finally the time came for me to leave for camp. Mom gave me the money to buy new underwear, socks, and a bathing suit for the trip. I told her my old bathing suit didn't fit anymore and chose a red one-piece suit that covered more of me. I put the clothes, two library books, a flashlight, and a comb into a small suitcase. The camp provided everything else, including books, but I thought I'd better bring my own, just in case. I couldn't go two weeks without reading at least two books. I was what people called a bookworm, which was a good thing, I thought.

Mom had to go with me to the pick-up place at the Vine Street School. I wore shorts and a tee shirt but she dressed more formally. She had rolled her stockings up and attached them to a girdle and wore white, lace-up old lady shoes. Because of the July heat, she wore a pale yellow sleeveless dress. A large blue-green bruise covered part of her right upper arm.

"Who did that? Daddy?"

"Mind your own business." Her face was powdered and rouged and her lips were dark red. Around the house she wore slippers and a house-dress and never did anything to her face at all. Now she looked respectable, like any other mother, and I was glad for that.

We took a bus down Albany Avenue toward downtown and transferred to another bus to take us up Vine Street. I would have walked the whole way but Mom was frail. She had bad varicose veins. I'd been born when she was thirty-five and there had been complications, what exactly I didn't know, but I knew from her stabbing remarks through the years that she blamed me for them. She seemed to blame me for lots of things, like her poor health, her moods, her lack of close family nearby. We didn't talk anymore until we were on the bus.

"You're more excited about camp this year than last."

"Because I know how much fun it'll be."

"You can thank your father for forcing you to go. Remember you wanted no part of it?" Her fingers brushed the bruise on her arm.

"I didn't know anything about it. And I didn't want to be an underprivileged kid."

"There's nothing wrong with that. There are more underprivileged kids in Hartford than there is space in that camp." We fell silent. I could smell whiskey on her breath and hoped others on the bus couldn't.

In the parking lot of the Vine Street School, the camp bus was loading passengers. Mom handed the admission letter to a counselor at the door of the bus. The bus was to leave at one-thirty, in just a few minutes. I kissed Mom's cheek, climbed into the bus and found a seat, and looked out the window to wave good-bye, but she was already walking back toward the bus stop. Maybe she wanted to get off her feet.

My mind drifted back a long time ago, to the summer I was seven, when Mom had taken me to a swimming pool across town so I could learn to swim. Every day until I knew the route well enough to go alone on my bike, we walked the long blocks down Woodland Street to Farmington Avenue. There we waited for a bus going downtown, and at Laurel Street, got off to transfer to another bus heading to Pope Park.

The trip took an hour. Mom sometimes had to stop and sit for a while on one of the low walls in front of the insurance companies lining the far end of Woodland Street or on the benches in the park. While I swam, she sat in the shade reading or talking with other younger mothers watching their toddlers play in the sandbox. She said the other mothers teased her about her Scottish accent.

Around three o'clock, we reversed the journey back to 416 Woodland. Usually Mom was tired and cross by the time we got home. She said the trip was too much to ask of someone who was forty-two years old. I started making the trip by myself after the first couple of weeks. At the end of the summer I got a certificate for having passed the advanced intermediate class.

Mom was pleased. "I've done my duty," she said.

Now I watched her walking slowly toward the Vine Street bus stop. There was no smell of whiskey on her breath back then. But now, as then, she would probably be in a bad mood by the time she reached home, ready to lash out at whoever came in her way.

CHAPTER 4

Times Farm

The camp bus chugged out of the paved schoolyard. Within half an hour we were across the Connecticut River and into farmland. My eyes were fixed on the passing scene. Our family didn't get out much anymore and I was hungry for each new sight. We passed tobacco fields covered with white cheesecloth and bordered by large, unpainted sheds where the tobacco was hung to dry. I knew about these shade-grown tobacco farms because Jacky and other older kids in the neighborhood talked about their summer work on them. Further on, corn and other crops spread out from both sides of the two-lane country road, ready for harvest. My cousins, who used to live out this way before they moved to California, said you could hear the corn growing. I didn't know whether that was really true. It sounded too weird, but nice at the same time.

The road narrowed and climbed upward into woods and dairy pastures. Pretty little houses, mostly white with black shutters and narrow front porches, were tucked into the woods or under a tree or two in the middle of a field. It would be nice to live out in the country like this, where everything was green and peaceful.

At a junction with a large sign announcing the name of the camp, the bus turned onto a dirt road shaded by a thick canopy of tall old trees that followed a river, which rushed gently over rounded rocks. I knew from last summer that this river was dammed further up to form a swimming hole. Chattering on the bus quieted as everyone's excitement about arriving took over.

The bus stopped alongside a grassy field with a flagpole. On one side was a large building that contained the dining hall and some offices. Off to the side were some smaller arts and crafts buildings and playing fields. Boys' cabins stretched toward the woods from the upper end of the far side of the parade field and girls' cabins stretched from the near side. In between were a glade of woods and some small utility buildings, toilets, shower rooms, and an open pavilion with a row of sinks and water fountains. It was all waiting just for us, the previous crop of kids having left just before we arrived. I felt comfort settling throughout my body to see it all again.

Laura, the counselor on the bus, was in charge of the senior girls' cabin, where I was assigned. It was last in a row looking out on thick woods. I had an upper bunk and could see the woods while lying flat. I arranged my books and the flashlight on a wood beam and put the rest of my stuff in a locker at the end of the bunk. Laura was rolling down the canvas shades over the screened upper half of the walls.

"C'mon girls, swimming test time. You need to change into your bathing suits."

"Already?"

"Yup, hurry up. We're the first ones but the other cabins will be lined up behind us."

Laura started getting undressed. Her breasts were large and full, white against the tan surrounding them, so different from Mom's. Laura had hair down below and wide rounded hips. She was not a child like most of us campers. I pulled on my new red bathing suit quickly, embarrassed about my thinness. Would I ever look like Laura? I had a bra, a 28 AA, swiped from the clothesline of Mrs. Shenk, who lived in my building, but I had put it aside for the summer, knowing I didn't really need it yet.

At the swimming hole, I passed the test that made me eligible to sign up for Junior Lifesaving. This river was clear and green, not brown like the Hog. Three other girls in my cabin would be in Junior Lifesaving with me and no one was from my school or even from my part of Hartford, the far northwest corner near the borders with West Hartford and Bloomfield. I fell asleep that night happy, looking forward to the days ahead.

We awoke at sunrise the next morning to the ringing of a distant, insistent bell, and washed with cold water at the outside basins. I used the toilet and flushed it by pulling a chain on an overhead tank that made enough noise to stir the bats nesting in the rafters. The woods were alive with bird songs and some of the campers competed with their own high-pitched giggles and shouts. This was the way I wanted to live, with laughter and happiness and the beauty of nature all around me, while doing worthwhile things, of course. Maybe I could be a camp counselor when I got older.

After pledging allegiance to the flag and hearing the program of the day, I trooped with everyone else to the dining hall for breakfast, the boys dressed in khaki shorts, tees, and sweatshirts stenciled with the camp's name, the girls in blue gym suits and the same sweatshirts. I liked being in a nice clean uniform, hiding my scruffiness.

The dining hall was warm and smelled of toast. As the line moved slowly forward, I talked excitedly about the day's program with Mary Jane, the girl in the bunk below me, particularly about the puppet theatre and Junior Lifesaving. This was Mary Jane's second time at the camp too. I noticed a boy several places in front of us who kept looking back, jabbing his finger toward us, smiling. I recognized him from Northwest, remembered his name: Charlie Something. He was new to the neighborhood, hadn't been in earlier grades with me, and was in the other sixth grade class, with Bobby. He probably knew about the Hog River. My happiness swooshed right out of me.

The boy got his breakfast and came back along the line to where I stood. He nudged my arm with his tray.

"You're from Northwest, aren't you?" The leer on his face made me freeze and I turned away. He leaned closer. "Yeah, you are. You're Cunty Kilgour. Remember the Hog River?"

Inching along with the line, I kept looking straight ahead. He kept pace with me, smirking, nudging, until I got to the narrow space in front of the food selections. He turned away then, with a last, honking, laugh and walked toward the tables. I wanted to smash his head with a tray. I stared at the food selections, my face burning, avoiding the curious looks of my cabin mates. Through blurred eyes I took the first food I saw, cereal, milk, and a banana and followed my group to a table.

"Who was that guy?" Mary Jane asked.

"No one worth knowing. He's a creep."

"Does he go to your school?"

"Yeah, but he's a trouble maker. Everyone ignores him. He always smells of pee."

I made that up without a qualm, protectively, so quick to lie that I surprised myself. No one said anything more and I was grateful for that. But all of the food tasted the same.

*   *   *

That one boy, an ugly boy with thin stringy hair hanging in his eyes, haunted me the whole two weeks and, to be honest, for a very long time afterward. He called, "Hey, Cunty Kilgour!" whenever he saw me. He told other boys. I could hear the words "Hog River," "stripped," "tits." I stared into the distance when I heard him, focusing on a tree or pretty scene if I could, or started a conversation with someone to block out the sound and the feelings that flared through me. He never approached me after the first time and no one else picked up on his calls. Girls who heard him asked what it was about and I said he was a liar and crazy. Maybe they could tell from my frozen face, the wave of heat that surely must have reddened my cheeks, that it was painful. They let it go. Laura never asked. Maybe she didn't hear.

Those two weeks were supposed to help me forget. But he seared the shame into my memory, forced me to put on a good face when I wanted to weep. When he wasn't around, I swam hard, furiously, and passed the Junior Lifesaving test. I received a badge to sew on my new red swimsuit.

I participated in all of the camp activities for girls in my age group and made friends with the seven girls in my cabin. Although I was closest to the ones in my swimming class, there were no cliques. We all got along.

I read four books and felt myself gaining weight and growing stronger. One night each week we went into the woods, made a campfire, and sang camp songs. On the two Sunday mornings, we went to the outdoor chapel in the pine trees, and it was as beautiful and peaceful as I remembered from the previous year. I tried to recapture the contentment I had felt there, but couldn't.

On the ride back into town at the end of camp, Charlie was on the same bus as I was. He didn't say anything but I sensed him looking at me from time to time. And I looked at him. He had a sour expression on his face and he was still ugly. I was about his size. Could I beat him up? I didn't know where he lived. Maybe I should follow him from the bus, grab his dirty dishwater hair, and pummel his face into the dirt. Would that make me feel better?

But when we reached Vine Street, Jacky was waiting for me, not Mom, and he had a serious, sad look on his face. I grabbed my suitcase, waved good-bye to my friends, and headed for my brother. The hell with Charlie, he wasn't worth it.

CHAPTER 5

Home

Jacky, three years older and my hero, seemed taller in only two weeks, and skinnier. His dark brown butch was shaggy around his face and ears, and he had circles under his brown eyes. He took my suitcase to carry. The older Jacky got, the less he hung around the neighborhood, or with me. I was glad to see him, more than I would have been to see my mother.

"Welcome home, kiddo. You want to walk or wait for the bus?"

"Let's walk. How come you're not at work with Daddy?"

"Lots of things have happened since you've been away, none of it good. Dad has had a bunch of doctor's appointments."

"For what? What's happened?"

"His heart trouble got so bad the doctors told him he had to quit working. He couldn't do the job anymore. You should see his ankles. They're so swollen you can't see the bones."

I trudged along beside him automatically, thinking about what he had said, remembering all the times the whole family had gone to Dad's work, a stockbroker's firm, to help him clean. He was the janitor, though I hated to tell people that. It was my job to sweep and mop the back stairwell and to clean the ladies' and men's rooms on the second-floor landing. Mom did all the dusting in the offices. Jacky helped Dad with everything else. He went almost every day after school and on Saturdays, unless he had some activity he couldn't get out of, like a church basketball game. I went with Mom most Saturdays. I wished now that I had gone the Saturday of the Hog River. My last chore of the day always was to sweep out the big garage in the basement with a push broom I could hardly lift. I didn't like working in the dark garage that smelled of oil and gas, especially because I was alone until Jacky finished upstairs. Once he joined me we finished fast, his tall frame moving his identical broom quickly forward and back in a martial rhythm he said was good for his muscles. As we neared the end, he sang cowboy songs.

My mother usually brought sandwiches, but sometimes we'd take a break and go to Connecticut Lunch down by the train station or to Goldstein's Delicatessen. Once in a while we'd work through the day and go to Honiss's Seafood Restaurant for supper. It was the only nice restaurant my parents ever went to, something about the fish reminding them of their childhoods in Scotland. I never knew when we'd go to Honiss's and it wasn't very often that we did. Dad drank steadily while he worked and usually wasn't in any condition to go to a restaurant at the end of the day. So we would go directly home, him driving slowly, haltingly, along the quiet early Saturday evening streets, the old green Ford filled with the smell of whiskey and cigarette smoke.

Jacky broke into my thoughts.

"He's tired all the time. It's been coming on slowly. Mom seems scared."

"What's going to happen if he can't work?"

"He talked with lots of people. They went to city hall to apply for welfare and then a city social worker came to the apartment."

I stopped in the middle of the side street. "We're going on welfare?"

He grabbed my arm and tugged me across the street to the sidewalk. "If we're lucky. First city, then aid to dependent children. That's you and me. They call it AFDC." He smiled, but it didn't reach his deep-set brown eyes.

I tried to absorb these facts and my feelings about them. I didn't know anyone on welfare, except maybe those black foster kids on Harrison Street. I thought it must be shameful. That's what Mom and Dad always said about people who didn't carry their own weight.

"Are they drinking more?"

He nodded. "Lots more."

We walked in silence for a while, until Jacky broke it. "How was camp?"

"It was okay, not as much fun as last year." I thought of Charlie, the Hog River, and looked sideways at Jacky as we walked along the treeless avenue. Did he know? The hot sun shimmered off the wide sidewalk and raised sweat on both our foreheads. We passed the Congregational Church, the Lenox Theatre, the shoe repair store, the insurance agent.

"What was different?" He didn't know, I was sure.

"Maybe I'm too old for camp. I made the age cut-off this year by only three months." I made my voice perkier, forcing the memory of Charlie deep into my mind. I didn't want to reveal the hurt to Jacky, to add to his worries. He wasn't very good at beating people up, even though he might offer to go after Charlie for me. "But I earned a Junior Lifesaving badge."

"Hey, now you can save me." He teased me, and I liked it. I always liked it. I did a little skip and stretched my stride to match his as we continued along Albany Avenue with its familiar landmarks, Dr. Felder's office, our church, the drycleaner, the Italian grocer, other small shops with apartments above them where some of our classmates lived, and finally the Esso gas station on the corner of our street. It felt good to be home, even though it wasn't as tranquil or beautiful as the countryside.

Mom and Dad were in the kitchen when we arrived. Mom was making shepherd's pie, one of her recipes from Scotland that we all liked. An aroma of meat and onions had greeted us in the hallway. Though all the windows were open, the apartment was hot. Cracked and torn shades on the living room windows, lowered to thwart the afternoon sun, flapped in the light breeze. I put my suitcase on my couch bed. In the kitchen, whose windows faced the driveway between 416 and 414 Woodland, it was even hotter. Smells of cigarette butts and smoke sullied the food aroma. A fan on the covered laundry sink pushed the hot mixture around the shabby room, bouncing it against the mustard-colored, grease-dusted walls, cutting the edge off my appetite.

Dad sat at the kitchen table in an old blue work shirt and stained khaki work pants, a bottle of Schaefer beer by his left hand, the one with the missing ring finger that he claimed had been amputated without anesthesia during the First World War, although he also admitted that his opponent in a fight stomped on it, crushing the bone, and all the anesthesia was being saved for soldiers. Dad was just a teenager then, but he said he was doing his part by working in Denny's Shipyard in Dumbarton, Scotland. I was never quite sure how much of his stories to believe. On good days he liked to spin a yarn about life in the old country or tease me about this or that. The teasing was a trait Jacky inherited. They both told me I was teasable and I always protested that I couldn't be, because I was a bookworm.

Mom's beer was at her place at the table, but she stood at the stove, an apron over her housedress, sprinkling paprika on the shepherd's pie. I kissed Mom's cheek, damp from the heat. "Smells good, Mom." She seemed sober, but didn't smile.

I walked around the table to Dad. "How are you, Daddy? Jacky told me."

He looked away from me, toward the small hallway that led to the bathroom and their bedroom and took a long drag on his Camel. He seemed pretty sober, too. "I'm fine, lass. The doctors say they're surprised I'm still alive. So that must be good, eh?"

He used my nickname, the Scottish word for girl, for the first time in quite a while. Mom never called me that; the nickname belonged to my father. I was Me to her and May to Jacky, and to most of the neighborhood, and even most of the time in school. No one called me Mary and that name sounded funny to my ear, as if it belonged to someone else. I touched his shoulder and leaned down to give him another kiss on his scratchy cheek. At that moment, I loved him intensely.

I sat in my chair, the one closest to the living room. Jacky was already across the table from me and handed over the bottle of milk. We ate tomato, cucumber, and onion salad with oil and vinegar, and my appetite returned. Had Mom prepared this good food to welcome me home? Unlikely. Maybe it was because of Dad's heart. Mom ladled out the shepherd's pie, sat again, and asked me how camp was. I said exactly what I had said to Jacky.

That evening I gave them gifts of Indian jewelry I had made at camp, key chains for Dad and Jacky, a bracelet for Mom, and a special birthday gift for Jacky: a picture of a ship burnt into wood with an electric burning pen. Jacky like ships and used to make models of them. I was happy when he said he liked it and would tack it to the living room wall next to his bed. We listened to the radio and Jacky and I played rummy, his rare company delightful, while Mom and Dad drank themselves to sleep.

*   *   *

Next morning I had a chance to see Dad's swollen ankles. He was having a hard time putting on his black dress shoes, so I helped him with the shoehorn and laced them for him.

"I need to go to Gourson's Drug to fill my prescriptions. Do you want to walk with me, lass?"

"Sure, Dad." I'd look for my friends later.

We walked the half block to the avenue and waited for the green light to cross the street. I noticed that my big toes had scratched through the tips of my blue Keds, new that spring. Had my feet grown that much during the summer? Dad always teased me about eventually having to buy shoes at a special canvas factory for people with big feet. Maybe he was right. I walked awkwardly beside him, thinking about my clodhoppers, out of step in part because he was walking slowly, though he was taller than I by six inches. Jacky was already the same height as Dad, almost six feet.

As we walked across the street, he glanced my way." Did Jacky tell you what the doctor said?"

"Yes, and about your job. And about the welfare."

"There wasn't anything else I could do, lass. My heart kept getting weaker and I kept getting more tired. Without Jacky's help this summer, I couldn't have done the job at all. And without your mother's and your help all this past year it would have been harder."

"What did the doctor say?" I heard a fearful edge creep into my voice.

"There's no cure but I can take medicines and I have to give up salt."

"Salt? But you love salt, and you eat a lot of it."

"I'm supposed to use a substitute but it tastes terrible." He chuckled. It sounded good.

In Gourson's, we had to wait for the prescriptions, so we sat at the counter. Dad ordered himself a ginger ale and me a root beer.

"So how was camp? You didn't say much last night. I guess you were tired, eh?"

"Yeah, I guess. It was good. I did a lot of new things. I was in a puppet show. I made a clown out of clay. We used a light bulb to shape the head." I felt I was talking about stupid, childish things.

"How did you do that?"

"We let the clay dry around the light bulb and then slit the clay in half to take the light bulb out. Then we put soft clay on the cut to seal it. After it dried again, we painted and dressed them up. Mine had an open mouth, a long nose, and hair of steel wool. Its part in the show was as a clown who was unhappy. The little kids liked the show."

"What else did you do?"

Did he really care about these things? "Well, I told you about the Junior Lifesaving. We had to stay in the water every day for an hour and a half more than the other kids and build up our stamina by swimming laps. We learned how to jump into the water without going under so we could keep our eye on the drowning person. After that we had to go in with all our clothes and sneakers on and take them off while staying calm. We practiced carrying drowning people through the water. I'm a strong swimmer now. I can save people if I have the chance, including myself."

"That's important."

I hadn't talked with my father like this in a long time and it felt odd. Conversation had become rare in our apartment. Usually, when drinking but not yet drunk, Dad swore at me; and he only called me lass when he liked me, which didn't seem very often. When he was drunk, he called me names like trollop and cunt, words that flew right over my head until the Hog River.

Mr. Levine, the pharmacist, called out, "Mr. Kilgour, your prescriptions are ready."

Dad got up to go to the back of the store. "Pick out a magazine for your mother," he said.

I found a new *Saturday Evening Post* and joined him at the counter. He paid and we went out into the heat of the city and walked home slowly. I carried the paper bag with his prescriptions and the magazine and kept myself to his slow pace, seeing the pain he was in from his tight shoes and who knew what else.

*　　*　　*

We went on welfare, as Jacky said. Soon, with nothing else to do, both Mom and Dad were drinking pretty much all the time and fighting with each other more and more, not just shouting but physical fights too, swinging and punching at each other when insults weren't enough. Sometimes I was smack in the middle of it. The welfare check wasn't very much, not enough to pay for all of our needs especially when they bought the liquor and cigarettes first. Before the end of the month there was nothing left.

A week before the September check was due the only food in the house was a large tin of sardines, some potatoes already soft and growing eyes, two packets of Kool-Aid, and some cereal but no milk. I opened the door to their bedroom and peeked in. Mom had an old housedress on but was still in bed. She looked at me through one half-opened eye. I walked toward the bed.

"Mom, there's nothing to eat in the house. Can you give me some money?"

"Don't bother me, I'm trying to sleep."

Dad opened his eyes. "Leave your mother alone, Me."

"Come on. You're still hung over from last night but I've been up for two hours and I'm hungry. It's already nine-thirty."

Mom stumbled out of bed surprisingly quickly and came at me swinging with her right arm and grabbing at my hair with her left.

"Buy some food with your allowance, you cheeky brat."

"Allowance? You haven't given me an allowance since we went on welfare! And you drink up the whole check." I fended off my mother's blows with my forearms, backing out of the room at the same time. "I should report you to the AFDC!"

I headed for the back door as I said this but Mom lunged for me and then Dad jumped up. Both of them started swinging and pushing me into the bathroom. I was three inches taller than my mother but it was trickier with Dad in the fray. His white boxer shorts bagged loose and dingy around his skinny legs, but he was still strong.

"Stop, let me go! I'm sorry, okay?"

"Cheeky bitch!" Dad took a quick swing that caught me on the ear.

"Ow! Okay, I didn't mean it. Let me out!" I was standing in the bathtub by this time.

"How dare you talk to us like that!"

Talk how? It was the truth. I screamed and shouted to distract them and then jumped up on the rim of the bathtub and vaulted between and past them.

"I hate you both!" I rushed through the narrow passage between the refrigerator and food cabinet in the hallway and out the back door, down the quiet corridor past the closed doors of the neighbors. I'd have to steal something if I wanted to eat. Stealing was wrong and dangerous, I knew, and that made me feel even worse.

CHAPTER 6

Child Abuse

On the first day back at school, it was pretty clear that seventh grade at Jones Junior High would be different from elementary school. Kids from two other elementary schools were joined with us from Northwest. Joanie and Stella were not in my homeroom. Joanie and I had only a history class together and I had no classes with Stella, but all three of us would be together in the afterschool sports program in the girls' gym. This was something new and I really looked forward to it.

But by the end of the first week or so, things calmed down. The afterschool sports program was every day from three to five P.M. and I made friends with a new girl in my homeroom, Brenda Lynch, who was a good basketball player. She was also in love with the best basketball player on the boys' varsity. I started going with her to the games in the boys' gym, listening to her love sighs and suggestive whispers. Desmond Keene was cute and nice, but I wondered whether he knew Brenda existed. Half the girls crowded together on the bleachers had a crush on him.

No one mentioned the Hog River. Lenore was still at Northwest, so I didn't see her at school, and I didn't see her around the neighborhood either. Joanie and Stella seemed to sense that the subject was off limits and said nothing about it. But my ears stayed permanently tuned to the awful words—Hog, stripped, raped, Cunty Kilgour—and my body tensed as I walked the crowded, shiny, wood-floored hallways between classes, especially when passing a group of boys. This moving from class to class was new. It meant we were trusted to get to our next class on our own. Some of the boys were already sneaking outside to have a smoke. I hadn't done that yet.

I never laid eyes on Bobby again. He must have left the orphanage. And I heard Charlie had stayed back, so he was stupid as well as ugly. Jimmy was around, even in two of my classes, but I tried to ignore him. His betrayal still burned.

Weeks went by. The hot weather was long gone. Afterschool basketball was proving to be the best thing about junior high. I was the captain of one of the six teams. I didn't get home until late afternoon, often after Mom and Dad were drunk enough not to notice whether I was there or not. I made my own supper and then hung around outside with the neighborhood kids or went to the library. Jacky wasn't around much.

In late October, the principal's office summoned me through a note to my teacher. As I walked down the empty corridor to the administrative offices, the floor creaked and my brain tried to think of what I had done that was bad enough to be called to the principal's office. The secretary's face revealed nothing as she directed me into the office of Principal Stanley, a man I had so far seen only on the auditorium stage and loping through the cafeteria on his long praying mantis legs.

"Sit down, Miss Kilgour," Mr. Stanley said. Oh, oh, this must be serious. He sat at a long table next to his desk. I took the seat he pointed to and noticed the school nurse, Miss Alcorn, who I knew from Northwest. Why was the school nurse here? Two other women—strangers—sat across the table from me. A queasy feeling gripped my stomach and spread upward.

"This is Miss Trent from the Department of Children and Families and this is Policewoman Black," he said, gesturing to the women.

A wind of dread seeped into me. Had they found out about the Hog River? Had my parents' drinking made them ineligible for the monthly welfare check? Had something happened to Daddy's heart since this morning, when I had left them still asleep from last night's drinking? Had something happened to Jacky? Oh, please God, let it not be Jacky.

Miss Trent spoke first. She was young, with old pimple scars on her cheeks. She smiled. "You're called May, right?"

I nodded, my head barely moving on my tensed neck.

"Well, May, we'd like to know how you're getting along at home."

I waited for her to say something more, to give me a hint as to how I should answer, but when she stayed silent, her face a mask, I said, "Okay." It came out almost like a squeak.

Miss Trent leaned across the table. "Is everything as it should be at your house?"

What was she getting at? How should it be at my house? My parents shouldn't drink and fight so much. My father should have a job. What else?

I shrugged stiff shoulders, looking at my long-fingered basketball-playing hands on the table rather than at any of them. "I guess so." I resisted the temptation to nibble on one of my nails. I wished I were playing basketball, running, catching, throwing.

The policewoman, prettier and bigger than Miss Trent, took over. "Some of your neighbors have told us about shouting and sounds of fighting coming from your apartment."

"Oh?" Maybe this wasn't going to be so bad. "My parents do shout a lot. Who complained?"

"We can't tell you that. But they're concerned about you, about your safety. Do your parents yell at you too?"

"Sometimes."

"Do they hit you?"

"Sometimes." I looked at the pictures on Mr. Stanley's wall.

"Do they hit you or spank you?"

My stomach muscles tightened. I didn't like the way this was going. What neighbor could have complained? Someone across the driveway in the next building, maybe those new people on the third floor I had seen peeking through their blinds? Someone from my own building, the parents of one of the kids I hung around with? And when? Both of my parents would smack me around if I did something to rile them and let them catch me. I usually didn't let that happen. But I remembered that big noisy argument when they trapped me in the bathroom. That was the loudest ruckus to come from our apartment recently that I could remember and my own shouts had been genuine, especially at one point when Mom had hold of my hair. Damn. I was partly to blame for this.

Waiting for an answer, the policewoman leaned back in her chair. Her gaze didn't waver. The normal outside world was pressing on my private, secret family world. I felt like a criminal, or an undercover spy caught by the enemy.

"They only beat up on me when I'm doing something wrong."

"How do they beat you?"

I didn't like that question. "What do you mean?"

"With open hand or fist?" An ominous feeling, silent and charged, took over the room. Their winter wool coats smelled of mothballs. Why were they doing this? What if I did tell them? What would they do? Arrest my parents? Send Jacky and me to the orphanage? Tell my parents and then do nothing? That would make things really bad, worse than now, if I told the outside world about our family things.

I lied. "Just slaps, open hand." My voice sounded strange to my own ears, flat and unconvincing.

"Why do you think the neighbors reported screaming and banging noises coming from your apartment? More than once."

I gulped in a deep breath. I had to fight back. "Because they're busy-bodies. Why don't they mind their own business?" I blurted out in a rush, "And why don't you mind your own business and leave my family alone?" I shivered and pulled my hands from the table into my lap, clenched into fists. I wished I could fly away from this stuffy, dangerous place right now.

The roly-poly nurse looked at the table instead of at me. Mr. Stanley looked out the window as if he wished he could fly away too, into the brisk autumn air. Neither of them intended to help me out here. The two strangers looked directly at me with unblinking eyes.

Miss Trent spoke. "Young lady, we're trying to help you. It's our job to investigate reports of child abuse and neglect."

They probably did this all day long, tormenting kids, trying to break up families. They were doing their jobs. They didn't care about me. Child abuse? I felt like an insect pinned under a spotlight for examination, a moth rather than a butterfly. An abused child. A neglected child. Was I? I felt too old to be a child.

"Well, you're not helping me. I can take care of myself. Just leave me alone!" I sensed my words might get me in more trouble but I didn't care. What right did they have to interfere?

The policewoman said, "May, tell us what's going on at home. If you don't tell us, we'll have to go over to Weaver and talk to your brother."

"Leave him out of this! He's in a new school. Don't ruin things for him!" The thought of Jacky being humiliated like this started me crying. He never got into any trouble, he wasn't around much, but they'd try to make him squeal on me and Mom and Dad. "There's nothing to tell. He won't tell you anything more than I'm telling you."

"You deny your parents are mistreating you?"

"Yes. I deny it. And tell whoever reported it to mind their own fucking business!" Oh, no, I hadn't meant to say that.

Mr. Stanley turned from the window. "Watch your tongue, young lady." He looked toward the policewoman. After a nod from her he said, "You may go now. The secretary will give you a pass."

Miss Alcorn got up and walked out of the room with me, handing me a tissue. I wiped the tears from my face and took the pass from the secretary. The nurse touched my shoulder but neither said a word and I looked away from them and walked into the still-empty hallway. I ached, like an old person, like my father.

I ducked into the girls' bathroom and washed my face, drying it with the rough brown paper towels. There was no time marked on the pass. I headed for the coatroom outside my homeroom to get my jacket. From there down the corridor into the part of the building that housed the elementary school, golden wood changed to brown linoleum and everything was closer to the ground. It made me feel as tall as a grown-up on the outside. Inside I felt little, and alone.

Passing my old fifth and sixth grade classrooms, then the fourth and third grades and the kindergarten, I left by the main door of the primary section. Up the street was Keney Park, woods whose trees already were dropping their leaves. I crunched through the newly dead ones and crossed the fading grass to the playground, already closed for the season.

Empty swings waited for me. I sat on a brown wooden swing seat, worn smooth and shiny by generations of kids, and the tears came again. I was furious with myself for crying in front of them, for letting them get to me.

Without a handkerchief or tissue, I sniffed hard and started the swing moving slowly to dry my cheeks. I knew one word in Spanish: *sobrevivir.* Survive. I may have learned it from a cowboy movie. But that's what I would have to do. Could I? I went faster and higher, pumping with all my strength, my body straight out, skirt billowing. My fists gripped the thick metal chain. The swing couldn't go any higher. On the last arc, when it reached its highest forward point, I jumped off feet first, flying through the air. I landed on loose, bent legs and rolled onto my side, curled up, like I was tumbling. The bare earth was harder than in summertime and it scraped the side of my knee enough to draw blood.

CHAPTER 7

Decline

The abuse people didn't visit Jacky at school, and I never figured out who squealed on us. Their visit stayed with me for years and I became conscious of every loud noise we made in the apartment and the danger that could come from it.

Things got worse and worse the longer Dad didn't work. Food was constantly scarce. Jacky, fifteen already, caddied on the weekends and set pins at night at a bowling alley downtown. Sometimes he set pins all night and didn't come home at all. Mom and Dad didn't notice or didn't care. But I always knew when he wasn't home. When he did come home, I tried to talk with him as much as I could. He had grown taller and stronger, proud of the hard muscles in his arms and stomach. I caught him sometimes flexing his biceps in the bathroom mirror and he invited me to punch him in the stomach as hard as I could, to prove his strength. He urged me to step on his stomach with bare feet and it was like stepping on a hard wobbly rock in a stream. I always did it reluctantly and stepped off gently for fear of hurting him.

Boys could do more things to earn money than girls. I babysat whenever asked by the neighborhood mothers, but that dried up as the weather turned cold. Lately I had taken to selling Christmas cards door to door but I wouldn't get any money until I delivered all the cards. I had to send people's down payments in with the orders. I roamed the neighborhood selling cards most nights and in December when the cards arrived I collected my commissions. Some of the kids at school collected for the March of Dimes and skimmed off some for themselves. I might do that after the Christmas card season.

I had my sales pitch down pat. "Good evening, I'm selling greeting cards. Would you like to see my samples? They're very nice and the price is good."

Sometimes they were curt: "No," and the door closed quickly. Sometimes I could smell cooking and wished they'd invite me in to join them. Other times they looked me up and down. I thought I might seem a little needy to them in my faded and worn flannel-lined jeans and thin school jacket. I knew I was skinny and my straight dirty blonde hair was a mess, pulled together in a ponytail that stuck out straight from my head. Some girls could get their ponytails to lie flat against their necks but mine wouldn't.

"Are you from around here?"

"Yes, I live on Woodland Street. My name's May Kilgour. I'm in the seventh grade at Jones."

"Oh, are you doing this for school?"

"No." Other people asked if it was for the Girl Scouts. "I'm doing it to earn spending money. There aren't too many jobs for girls, you know."

That usually got me invited to sit down and open the big book of samples I lugged with me.

It surprised me that so many people trusted me with down payments and my promise to return with their cards. And, while I stole food and sometimes other things from stores in the neighborhood without thinking too much about it, I was scrupulously honest with my greeting card business.

I delivered all the cards and got my money the week before Christmas. At Kamin's Five and Dime I bought Jacky a plaid flannel shirt to replace the one he had whose sleeves were so short that he had to keep them rolled up. I bought Dad a carton of Camels and Mom a box of chocolate-covered cherries at Gourson's Drug and still had twenty dollars left. My parents gave me five dollars from the welfare check. Jacky gave me a pair of warm, gold-colored mittens and a matching hat, and put a new two-dollar bill in each mitten.

"Merry Christmas, kiddo," he said to me with a yawn before he even rose from the three couch cushions on the floor that he used for a bed.

"Merry Christmas to you, too." I snuggled under my blanket on the couch across the room. I already knew what my gifts were and there was no tree, no particular reason to get up.

We didn't do or eat anything special on Christmas Day. Dad sat at the kitchen table for most of the morning, smoking and drinking beer.

"Where's Mom?" I asked, making toast for Jacky and me.

"In bed, resting."

"Is she sick?"

"No. It's probably the change of life." He said that a lot, as if it explained everything. I knew a boy from around the corner whose mother stayed in bed all day every day, in a nice bedroom in a nice house. She invited visitors in, even the neighborhood kids, and was said to be going through the change of life.

Jacky went to the bowling alley in late afternoon to set pins. I read for a while then listened to the radio from under the blanket in my bed to escape the cold in the apartment. But I was wide awake. I tried to think of all the good things that had happened in my life, starting with previous Christmases, remembering the year I had gotten the doll and the toy gas station and hadn't found either of them before Christmas morning. I remembered summer times. Sundays at Batterson Park had been nice. The beginnings of those days were good. Dad would rent a boat and brag he still rowed as well as he had in his youth in Scotland on a rowing team. But he drank steadily in the boat and later while he cooked the hamburgers at the picnic grove. On the ride home, he could hardly drive in a straight line and went more slowly than the other drivers. Mom sat in front, sleepy and silent from her own drinking. Jacky and I would sink down in the back seat so no one could see us and plait lanyards from flat, plastic string called gimp that we bought at the five and dime store.

Well, that counted as only half a good memory. I turned over carefully to avoid a broken spring and stretched my memory further, to a lake where we rented a cottage. Dad came there only on weekends. He would bring taffy and hide it all over the rambling old house so Jacky and I would search for it while he and Mom slept in. Those vacations had been peaceful. Jacky and I roamed the woods surrounding the lake, swam by ourselves while Mom sat on the beach reading or talking with other adults. Sometimes she gave us money to buy grape sodas and chocolate cupcakes at the little store next to the beach that smelled of fish and ripe fruit. Once Jacky chased me with a garter snake he had caught until Mom made him stop. Once he cut his head when the hatchet fell off its handle while he was chopping wood. Mom had to press on it with a towel to stop the bleeding. Forever after he had an inch-long scar on the back of his head where no hair would grow. The rented cottage was clean and old-fashioned, with a pump in the kitchen and cubbyholes in the walls for hide and seek. The memory of that lake was so vivid we must have gone there several times. Or could it have been only once? Childhood memories stick to the bones so tightly they make the adult. It was especially important to remember the good ones, to become a good adult. I wondered where I had learned that. Maybe from Mom and Dad, who talked often of growing up in big families in Scotland. Mom had so many sisters that one of them was given to a childless aunt and uncle. But she was taken back when Mom's family had to go to Canada because her father's political activities got him in trouble.

*   *   *

One night toward the end of the school year, shouting and swearing from my parents' bedroom woke me up. But I soon fell back asleep. The next morning, Jacky and I left for school while our parents slept. That evening when I came home from basketball, Dad was sitting at the kitchen table trying to wrap a gauze bandage around his arm. He was drunk and couldn't put it on straight.

"What happened, Dad?"

"Your mother bit me, the bitch."

"She bit you? Should I look?" He nodded. I unrolled the bandage to see an oval of pulpy red-black mush surrounded by a rim of angry red skin. "Ugh. This looks serious, Dad. What made her bite you?"

"I don't know. I think I rolled over and touched her in my sleep. She must be having a nervous breakdown with this change of life. See if you can find some ointment to put on it, lass."

I went to the bathroom medicine chest and came back with Vaseline. "This is all I could find. Will it work?"

"Let's try it." I put some Vaseline on the gauze with a knife and wrapped the rest of the gauze around his arm, cutting the end into two halves with the scissors to tie it. I heated a can of Campbell's mushroom soup and split it with him for our supper. Jacky didn't come home that night.

But the ointment didn't cure Dad's arm. It might even have made it worse by cutting off the air, but I didn't know that at the time and neither did he. Over the next several weeks it definitely got worse and started to smell. You could tell where he was in the apartment by the strength of it. We opened all the windows to shoo it out. This cured me of ever wanting to bite anyone and convinced me I could never become a nurse.

Mom moped and claimed she couldn't remember biting him. Why would she bite her own husband, she asked each of us in turn? I gritted my teeth and frowned. Dad accepted her explanation, no longer angry. But he said the pain spread up his arm and penetrated deeper into it. Even though Mom washed it with peroxide every day, the wound turned gray-black and stayed mushy. With the bandage off, the stench was of something terribly rotten. He had an appointment with his cardiologist the next day and said he'd ask him to look at his arm.

The next afternoon he walked in the door ashen-faced from the physical effort of the trip downtown to the doctor and from the news he had gotten: He had gangrene.

"He took one look at my arm and sent me to a surgeon in the same building. He didn't even check my heart."

"What'd the surgeon say?" asked Jacky, who was home for some reason.

"I'm in danger of losing my arm unless the antibiotics stop the infection. He cleaned the wound and gave me these sample medicines, the prescriptions, and the rest of this." He pointed to a pile of bandages, and a list of instructions on the table. "He told me to come back every two days so he could treat the wound himself."

"Did he ask how it happened?" Jacky's voice sounded tight.

"Only how on earth I had gotten such a wound outside of wartime." Mom and Dad exchanged a glance. "Don't worry, I told him I cut it on the edge of a sharp machine. He seemed to believe me."

Jacky snorted but said nothing and walked into the bathroom. Our family secrets were safe.

For the next month it was touch and go. Mom changed the dressing every day after the first week of the doctor's care, handling Dad's arm gently, following the doctor's instructions, nicer to Daddy than she had been for a long time. Eventually his arm healed completely and they settled back into their old fighting and drinking routine.

*   *   *

I was sorry to see seventh grade end. I liked school. I fooled around, never studied, and played hooky quite a bit, and came home with passing grades in everything. But the summer was nice, too, and passed pleasantly. I preferred warm weather, always. It was just easier to live when the weather was gentle. Too old for camp, I hung around with Joanie and Stella or with the neighborhood kids, playing baseball with a tennis ball in the backyard or cards and Monopoly on the front stoop or back porch. Sometimes we practiced somersaults on the big lawn of the house next door, where my friends Annie and Paula lived. I babysat almost every morning, mostly a difficult toddler I took to the park and kept occupied with the baby swings and by feeding him animal crackers, eating a lot of them myself. Every few days I went to the library, sat reading in its comfortable air-conditioned rooms, and checked out another book to take home. I read *Black Beauty* for the third time; *A Girl Called Hank,* about a tomboy like me; and *A Tree Grows in Brooklyn* by saying it was for my mother. I read so many books so fast that I forgot them as soon as I returned them to the library, hungry for more.

I ran errands for neighbors and collected empty soda bottles to turn in to the Popular Market for refunds of two cents or a nickel. I lifted many of these bottles at night from the back porches of my neighbors and bought things to eat with the change I rustled up: penny pretzels and strings of black licorice, potato chips, Cokes, and Popsicles.

I tried to keep my home life separate from everything else. I was pretty friendly in the neighborhood and was usually chosen as one of the leaders in our sports matches, but at home I found myself turning surly. Best to stay away as much as possible, I told myself.

CHAPTER 8

The Leather Coat

In the middle of eighth grade, in the dead of a cold January night in 1954, when things in the country were supposed to be good, I was sleeping on my couch without cushions pushed tight against the living room wall. I woke instantly and stiffened as Mom stumbled into the room, banging against the sofa, muttering. This had happened before, so I knew what was coming next, but it didn't dull the pain as she yanked my hair and snatched away my blanket. I reached for my head and leaned toward her to ease the pain. She let go and turned away.

"Ungrateful bitch. It's because of you I lost my health."

I watched her disheveled shadow stumble back through the kitchen and hallway into the bedroom beyond and slam the door. The apartment became dark again and I could hear Jacky, on the other side of the room on his bed of loose cushions, turn over and sigh.

"Are you okay?" he asked.

"Yeah, but she took my blanket." I lay curled up for a while longer until the cold penetrated my pajamas.

"I hate her."

"Use Dad's leather coat. Or I'll get it and you can have my blanket."

"It's okay."

I got up and silently slipped into the kitchen to the closet that held the junk of our family's life. From a hook on the back of the door I lifted Dad's ancient and worn brown leather overcoat. It

45

smelled of him as I remembered from my early childhood. There were still shreds of tobacco in the pockets. I went back to my bed and covered myself with the coat, bending my legs to fit my body under the coat's bulk. From the sound of his breathing, Jacky had fallen back asleep. He had been out all night for the past two days at his bowling alley job. He sometimes was able to sleep there.

I thought back to when I had my appendix out in the third grade. Mom had been nice to me then, crying in the emergency room when the doctor told her my appendix had already burst and I had to go right then to the operating room. Her Scottish brogue became so thick the doctor couldn't understand her and I had to repeat her questions to him. Her hand holding mine became wet as she walked beside the stretcher on wheels as far as they would let her go.

Another time, on Jacky's birthday, we decided to make a cake. Other kids seldom came into our apartment, which was shabby and dirty compared to their homes, but this time we had cleaned for Jacky's birthday and Mom let me invite Sheila from next door to help us. When it came time to frost the cake, Mom couldn't find the cake decorator and said she would use waxed paper instead. When the frosting started oozing out, I thought it was a mistake and cupped my hands around the opening to catch the frosting. Mom laughed so hard she couldn't explain that the funnel was working. That made me start laughing, and Sheila joined in. With all of the frosting in my cupped hands and the funnel empty, Mom explained. We continued to laugh and joke as we scooped the frosting back into a new funnel Mom made and she guided it onto Jacky's cake in swirls and curls. She didn't turn nasty at all that afternoon and later Sheila said my apartment wasn't that bad after all and that my mother seemed nice. I nodded, as if it was like that all the time.

There were other times in my thirteen years when my parents showed they loved me. Especially Dad: when he bought Jacky and me bikes at the same time, rather than making me wait three years so we'd get the bikes at the same age, like he had done with our signet rings. I loved that blue Monarch bike and rode it everywhere from the age of six until someone stole it at Pope Park when I was eleven.

I remembered the Friday evenings after work when Dad took me to the old storefront library and used his card to check out picture books for me until I got my own card and could do it myself. He waited for me without complaining while I studied all the books before selecting the few I could take home. Then I wondered why they seemed boring at home, not realizing at the time that it was because I had already 'read' them. That memory was going way back, before first grade, maybe before kindergarten.

I used to sit on the edge of the bathtub and watch Dad shave, talking with him while I watched. And he would sit on the hamper and let me comb his hair, arranging the sparse gray strands across the top and smoothing the fringe along the sides and back.

What else? Tomorrow I'd ask Jacky what good times he remembered. I'd ask him why things were so bad now and what he thought was going to happen next.

It was cold in the apartment. The stove must have run out of kerosene. Against the glow from the streetlight the frost on the front windows looked like silhouettes of mountain peaks in a full moon. I tucked my head beneath Dad's old coat and put my hand into the pocket to feel the tobacco.

CHAPTER 9

Making Do

A few days later, Jacky and I walked to school together.

"Do you have any money, May?"

"Are you kidding? Not since I spent my last babysitting money a week ago."

"Here, take this." He handed me three dollars. "I made some good tips. I'm going to bring home some groceries from the store after work tonight. Will you be there?" He had been working part-time at the First National since he turned sixteen the previous summer and kept doing the caddying and pin setting as well.

"For sure, if there's food."

He gave my arm a soft punch and walked toward the high school a block up the street, his shoulders in his brown leather Eisenhower jacket hunched against the late winter cold, his skinny legs hidden by thick brown corduroy pants.

I tucked the three dollars into my mitten and joined the kids streaming into Jones.

After homeroom, walking to my first class, Stella Pagano called to me.

"Hey May. Wait up," Stella, a pretty mixture of an Irish mother and an Italian father, had been in first grade with me, but we had only become close friends in the fifth grade. She lived about three blocks down toward Vine Street. "You ready for Saturday?"

"Yeah. Where're we going?"

"Probably Fox's. They've got the best stuff."

"Yeah, but they've also got more sales people."

"Nothing happened last time, did it?"

I shrugged as we took our seats. Joanie Dresser would go with us, although I never could figure out why Joanie stole things when she already had such nice clothes. Mr. Krantz, the history teacher, began talking and the room quieted. He handed back a test. I got a B. I thought about the three dollars in my pocket. Now I'd have enough for bus fare and for lunch downtown tomorrow. I hated it when the other kids had to lend me money, knowing I probably wouldn't pay it back.

At lunch in the cafeteria I sat with Joanie, Stella, Brenda, and some other girls from the Cool Cats basketball team. I took out the peanut butter and jelly sandwich I'd brought from home and the half pint of milk I'd bought. My stomach gurgled from this first food of the day.

After school, I went to the girls' gym to play basketball. I loved that gym in the attic of the school, with its soft, rust-colored linoleum floor, soaring roof, smells of leather and rubber and dry, dusty heat, and the sounds of balls bouncing and girls shouting. Skylights in the roof let in shafts of light on sunny days. The Cool Cats, my team, was one of the best in the school. I liked most sports, but I loved basketball. I was already five foot seven and fast on my feet.

From the gym I went to Maxwell's drug store in the shopping center near the corner of Blue Hills Avenue to see if I could steal myself a candy bar to last me until supper. The clerk watched me like a cop so I paid for a Hershey bar and ate it slowly, letting each square melt in my mouth to stretch the pleasure as I looked through the magazines.

Next I headed to the library. I wouldn't be eating anything else until Jacky came home after nine o'clock. There was no point in going home earlier, when my parents would be at their worst: half awake and drinking.

Our new neighborhood library, just down from Northwest, was shiny bright, the tables smooth and unmarked. Some adults and high school kids sat in the main reading room. Two smaller rooms for elementary and junior high kids were empty. I walked toward the new book display in the junior high room. Mrs. Floyd, the librarian who was as tiny as a child but dressed and acted like an adult, caught my eye and motioned me to the front desk.

"We have a new book that might interest you. I saved it for you." She reached under the desk and retrieved a thin dark blue book.

I touched the weave on the cover with my fingers, curious about what its small size could hold, thanked Mrs. Floyd and went into the junior high room. For the next three hours, interrupted only by a bathroom break and a few whispered conversations with kids coming and going, I read about a girl who lived through many hardships in colonial times, a good combination of history and story. Finished, I returned it to the front desk.

"Thanks for saving this for me, Mrs. Floyd. I liked it."

"You're finished already? Pretty soon we're going to run out of books for you!"

I flashed the dimple in my right cheek. People seemed to like dimples and often commented on mine. "Then you'll have to let me into the adult section."

Mrs. Floyd laughed without making a sound. "We'll have to see about that. Good night, dear."

In her quiet way, always speaking just above a whisper, Mrs. Floyd was one of my favorite people. Even when she had to kick the kids out of the library for making too much noise, she did it apologetically, as if it was a sin to have to banish us from books. She was especially nice to me when I was alone. I wondered if she had children of her own.

Just before nine I started along the avenue to Woodland Street, hurrying in the cold, gloomy weather. The last of the stores was closing. I huddled inside my green jacket with the two big gold J's sewn on it, pulling the fabric close to my body with pocketed hands. My feet in Keds and thin socks felt the cold first. I had rubber boots but there was no snow yet, so it would look funny to wear them.

Coming up to our old yellow brick apartment building, I looked up at the second floor right, at the two front windows in our living room. A dim light showed, possibly meaning that my parents were still not drunk enough to have gone to their bedroom to sleep or that Dad was sleeping in his chair in the kitchen. I went into the narrow tiled front vestibule with its wall of twelve brass mailboxes, and bent to reach my hand through a broken window to open the locked front door. I climbed the dim stairway, making little noise on the black ribbed rubber matting. At our door, I listen. Hearing nothing, I opened the door softly, snuck in, and closed the door just as quietly.

It was the light in the kitchen that was on. Sure enough, Dad sat in his chair at the table in his underwear, sound asleep, somehow keeping his balance. A half-empty glass of whiskey sat on the table along with an ash-tray full of cigarette butts. He snored and a string of mucous hanging from his nose swayed with each breath. I looked away.

Mom was not in the kitchen and I hoped she was already asleep behind the closed bedroom door. Dad was usually benign, but Mom was unpredictable and violent when she was drunk. I had been bonked on the head without warning too many times, once, in front of a friend, with a thick wooden cutting board that made me see stars. Alcohol affected my parents differently and I was always wary around my mother. No bites for me, thank you.

Moving carefully to not wake anyone, I went into the bathroom to wash some underwear that had been soaking and then hung it from the clothesline rope strung over the bathtub. I took the full wastebasket from the bathroom, combined it with the full one in the kitchen, grabbed a flashlight, and took the trash to the garbage shed in the backyard. If Jacky was bringing food home, the least I could do was straighten up a little. I returned to the apartment as quietly as I had left. I saw none of the neighbors, although I could smell their suppers as I passed each door, spaghetti sauce, roasted meat, something tangy and mouth-watering. Hunger pangs hit my stomach and I wondered what food Jacky would bring.

It was cold in the apartment. I gently shook the kerosene container that fed the stove, our only source of heat. Empty. I'd wait until Jacky got home and ask him to go to the cellar with me to fill it. Even though we kids played in the cellar on rainy days and I had perfected my ability to smoke down there with Annie from next door, I hated going down there at night. It was even worse than the garbage shed for spookiness. Besides, I couldn't lift the full container, a bottle inside a metal casing, and put it back onto its stand upside down without using both hands and my body, which got me covered with kerosene. And I worried that I'd do it wrong and blow us all up.

Jacky came through the living room door, and I motioned him to be quiet, pointing first to Dad and then to the bedroom. Jacky put a brown paper grocery bag on the kitchen table and started taking things out. First came two big, Italian sandwiches called grinders from Rosie's Pizza Parlor. I recognized them immediately, before their scent reached me, and my stomach started to rumble. Next he pulled out two quarts of milk. The rest of the bag held the food we'd eat in the coming days. I watched him unpack it all, each soft thud and crinkle threatening to wake Dad: a loaf of bread and cans of chicken gravy, tuna fish, Vienna sausages, corned beef, lima beans, spinach, condensed milk, jars of applesauce, peanut butter, grape jelly, and a small one of mayonnaise.

Without Jacky, I'd have to steal food as well as clothes. I wished I were sixteen and could get a real job. The babysitting around the neighborhood wasn't steady. The greeting card company had gone out of the door-to-door business. I had asked about a paper route, only to be told they didn't take girls. I shoveled snow when I could, but that was less steady than babysitting. Occasionally a neighbor in the next building, Mrs. Jones, would give me money to run errands. She was blind and her own daughter, Nancy, even older than Jacky, wasn't home much anymore. Sometimes Mrs. Jones would tell me to buy a big Hershey bar and we'd sit in her kitchen or on the porch in nice weather and I'd read the weekly magazines to her. Between us we'd eat the whole Hershey bar. Mrs. Jones would ask me about school and sports and reading, and sometimes about my mother, but not in a prying way. Mrs. Jones had her chair permanently on the porch but I sat on the rough wooden floor, my back against the brick wall, the sun warming us as I read to her or as we talked. This was a good memory to put on my list.

Jacky and I stuffed ourselves, each eating a whole grinder packed with Italian meats, provolone cheese, tomatoes, lettuce, roasted peppers and sprinkled with oil and spices. I pointed to my stomach and smiled at him as I finished off my milk.

"Boy, was I hungry."

He smiled back but turned serious as he looked at Dad, still sleeping sitting up. I watched my brother's face and thought it showed annoyance, or maybe disapproval. It was hard to tell exactly what.

He got up and jerked his head toward the living room. I followed him, closing the door behind me. He slouched into Dad's brown striped chair in front of one window and lit a Lucky Strike cigarette. One of his long legs hung over the arm and still almost touched the floor.

"You want one?"

I nodded. He tossed me the pack and his Zippo lighter and I lit one too, sitting in my mother's smaller green chair in front of the other win-

dow. The only light in the room came from a streetlight and from our cigarettes, which flared with each drag. A piece of tobacco stuck to my lip and
I spat it into the dark space. I usually smoked filtered. We both looked out
at the quiet street, lined with tall elm trees whose leaves in summer turned
the street into a shady green tunnel. Now the trees stood in a row like
skeleton soldiers, dark brown against cloudy black.

"What've you been up to?" His voice was low.

"Nothing much," I whispered back. "My team won our game today. I
got twenty points."

"That's pretty good."

"How about you? How's eleventh grade?"

He shrugged. "Boring." He was less interested in school than I was.
And he didn't like to read. I couldn't figure that out. Maybe it was because
he was a boy and worked all the time. Whenever he brought a book home
from his English class I'd read it and tell him what it was about: *David
Copperfield, Hiroshima, A Tale of Two Cities*, all much more interesting
than the eighth-grade anthology we had to read.

"Jacky, we need to get some kerosene. The container's empty and the
stove's out."

"Okay. I'll do it."

"I'll come with you and help you carry it. I don't like to go down there
by myself."

"Why? Are you scared? You don't believe Dad's old stories about the
boogie man, do you?"

"Well, there could be somebody there." Since the Hog River I had
become aware of danger. But Jacky still didn't know. At least, we never
talked about it.

"You're right, let's go. I may need protection." It was okay for him to
tease me. I liked it as long as he didn't think I was a chicken.

He retrieved the container from the kitchen. The long cement corridor in the cellar filled with shadows from the lights I turned on. Our cubi-
cle was in the darkest part, where the smell of dust and cat pee was
strongest. But I wasn't afraid with Jacky there. He opened the locked door
with the key we kept on the ledge above the door, filled the can from a
large drum, using a pump attached to a flexible metal hose, then wiped his
hands and the top of the can with a rag hanging from a nail on the wall

behind the drum. A man who supplied the entire building filled the drum through the window. We had managed to pay his bill and the drum would last the winter.

We both grabbed hold of the now full can. The narrow wire handle cut into my hand and the stink of kerosene was strong.

"It'd be easier if I carried it myself."

"But I want to help."

"Okay, but bend your arm a little so I don't have to stoop so much."

We made our way to the second floor, knocking the can into each other's legs on the narrow stairs. After Jacky lifted the heavy can upside down, hooked it to the stove, and made sure the kerosene was flowing, we got ready for bed, turning our backs to each other to undress. He slept in jockey shorts and a tee shirt, I in old pajamas that were too short for me. Since my blanket was still missing, I got the leather coat from the closet again. I hoped this night would be peaceful, that my mother would leave me alone. It wasn't exactly a prayer that I said, but maybe close.

"Night, Jacky." But he was already asleep.

I thought about how good the grinder and milk had tasted and about how I'd eat the rest of the food Jacky had brought home, sometimes with him, sometimes alone. After that, if the AFDC check hadn't come, I'd steal what I had to, or try to get invited to other people's houses.

CHAPTER 10

Stealing

On Saturday morning, I met Stella and Joanie at Gourson's Drugstore. We read true love magazines and talked to other kids for a while before going to catch the bus for downtown. It was eleven o'clock. The bus drove down Albany Avenue, out of our immediate neighborhood through an Italian area, one mostly of Puerto Ricans, then into one mostly of blacks as we traveled the two or three miles to downtown. The edges of the neighborhoods blurred: the Italian grocery store in our mixed neighborhood, the kosher supermarket with the Puerto Ricans, the black area mixed with the start of downtown, and the Italians near the Connecticut River. There was no Scottish neighborhood that I knew of.

We got off the bus and ran through the cold into Hartford's best department store, G. Fox. At one time, Dad had worked for the bank that managed the owner's country estate. I remembered visiting it once with him, to change light bulbs in the barn with a long pole. That was back when he had two jobs, before drinking took so much of his time. The family must have been very wealthy to have a bank change their light bulbs. I figured they wouldn't miss the things I stole from their store, although maybe I thought that just to make myself feel better about it.

It was easy. I took several skirts and sweaters into the dressing room to try on, making sure to stay in the dressing room long enough to try on all the clothes, in case someone was watching. But I quickly decided I liked a gray pleated skirt best. I hoisted it to my chest and zippered it enough that it wouldn't slip down. I pulled my jeans on over the skirt, folding and smoothing out the skirt fabric carefully to lay flat. My shirt and jacket helped hide the added bulk. I carried out the other clothes and carefully put them back in their right places. Stella came out of her dressing room and repeated the same thing. We talked back and forth that we hadn't found the exact item we wanted. I held up one sweater and said I liked it but it was too tight.

"Your tits must be growing fast," Stella retorted.

"Shut up, someone could hear you!" I frowned, but it was part of the game, to deflect attention from the loot we had under our clothes. It was really shameful the way we did it, but funny too.

"Where's Sue? I wonder if she found anything." I referred to Joanie by her alias. We each had one, in case of trouble. I was Helen Gallagher.

Joanie came out of the dressing room and followed the same routine.

"I like this one but it's too expensive. I'll have to ask my father first if I can buy it. But I'm hungry. Let's go eat." Her voice was taut with acting. Joanie's father was dead.

Now began the scariest part: walking through the store and out into the street. If we were going to be caught, it would be outside. That had happened once to me; the store manager had snatched the ID bracelet off my wrist and growled at me to stay out of his store. But he let me scurry away. It left me shaken and embarrassed, and I swore to steal only essentials from then on.

The three of us rode the escalator to the ground floor and sauntered along, stopping to finger gloves and handbags and once to spray each other with perfume. We followed this slow pace when we really wanted to run like hell. We reached the revolving doors and went out onto the sidewalk. Throat tight, arms tense, I tried to loosen up as we walked toward the end of the block, but a man in a security uniform standing at the corner stiffened me up again. He looked at us and then behind us. Stella looked back and motioned for us to stop and look at one of the windows. As we stood looking at a bunch of towels and bed sheets, I peeked back to see a woman without a coat standing at the store's main door. Had she been communicating with the security man?

"Just act normal. Keep walking. If they're going to get us, they'll do it at the corner."

I could hear Stella muttering under her breath. "Oh, God. My father's going to kill me, he's going to kill me."

"Act normal. We haven't done anything, have we?" I laughed to encourage them and confuse the security man.

At the corner, we waited for the light to change. The man didn't approach us. I wanted to run but knew I had to stay calm and look innocent. We reached the other side of Main Street and walked along a narrow side street lined with smart shops. At the next corner we turned and stopped at a store window to look back. The security man was gone.

"Whew, that was fun!" Joanie laughed. "I made a good haul: two pairs of slacks and a sweater. Let's go to the White Tower for lunch."

Stella laughed, her father's ire forgotten. "I got two sweaters!"

"I got one skirt for all that!" And I didn't think it was fun.

After lunch, we took the bus back to our neighborhood. Stella went home but I stopped at Joanie's house and was happy to be invited to stay for supper. This often happened. I ate a couple of meals a week at Joanie's house and stayed the night once or twice. The house was large and Joanie had the whole attic to herself, plus a regular bedroom on the second floor. Her mother had moved back in with her parents when Joanie's father was killed in World War II and then inherited the house when her parents died. Mrs. Dresser always made me ask permission from my parents to stay overnight. I used to pretend to dial and talked into a dead phone, dutifully asking permission from no one. After the telephone company cut off the phone, and we became the only people without one, which Joanie and her mother knew, I had to pretend I walked home to ask my parents' permission. I would just go around the block and come back to Joanie's, saying it was okay. That's what I did on this night. Joanie's mother never questioned the charade, although I thought she saw through it. She never even said anything about us not having a phone. I was thankful she didn't say anything. I liked sleeping in their attic. It was warm and Joanie and I slept in a big, comfortable, clean double bed. Mrs. Dresser never yelled at Joanie, at least in front of me.

Joanie and I went up to the attic as soon as we could to take off our stolen clothes. She had a hiding place in an unused corner where she stashed things until she gradually introduced them into her wardrobe. Joanie was shorter and plumper than I was but we could wear each other's clothes and often did. If her mother ever asked about a new outfit, Joanie could say she borrowed it from me or one of her other friends. Planning to take my new skirt home tomorrow, knowing my parents would be oblivious, I folded the skirt nicely to reduce the wrinkling. We spent the rest of the evening watching television, eating popcorn and drinking cider. I felt safe after the scare from the security man, and comfortable and warm in Joanie's house.

CHAPTER 11

Church

The next morning, I left for home when Joanie and her mother left for church. I lived around the corner, toward the end of our long block, and I usually took the most scenic route home: through Joanie's yard into other people's backyards, and through a vacant field behind the dry cleaning plant we called Nicky's after the janitor. I climbed over a tall picket fence to reach the alley between the garages belonging to my apartment building and the brick wall of a moving and storage company warehouse owned by Annie and Paula's family.

Remembering that Jacky might be home on a Sunday morning, I shuffled through the tall weeds until I came to the window of my family's garage. I pushed up the unlocked window and lifted myself through it onto a shelf Dad had built. From there I climbed over his 1937 Ford's green hood to reach the narrow space between the car and the wood-and-chicken-wire wall of our garage. It smelled of stale air and engines and a hint of stink from the garbage shed next door. I opened the back car door and put the stolen skirt under the front seat. I sat for a while, thinking, skimming through the old newspapers piled on the floor. The yellowed, brittle front pages had stories about the Korean War, the Communists, Senator McCarthy and Congress, and the anniversary of the big Hartford circus fire. Except for the circus fire, none of it affected me at all. I was supposed to go to that circus but Jacky had the mumps and it was so hot that Mrs. Jones said she'd rather take Nancy and me to the movies. I remembered Dad taking an interest in all of this news. Maybe he put the papers in the car. I had already read all the comic sections more than once.

The car, which didn't work anymore and sat idle in the garage, was my safe place, my refuge. I often slept in it, using the newspapers as a blanket, when things in the apartment got bad. But today, hoping it would be too early for that, I climbed back out the window and went along the alley to a narrow side path that led into the graveled backyard. As I went up the back stairs to Apartment 2D, all was quiet. I opened the door without making a sound.

Jacky was getting dressed. "Hey, where've you been?"

"At Joanie Dresser's. Where're you going?" He had on his best clothes.

"Church. Want to come? You can sit with me and my friends."

"I can? They won't mind?" These older kids usually ignored me. "But I don't have anything to wear." I should have brought the skirt with me from the garage, although I wouldn't have wanted to explain to Jacky where it came from. It still had the price tags on it. He'd notice much more than Mom or Dad would, although maybe he'd understand.

"Wear something from school."

"Okay. Wait for me." I pulled the skirt and blouse I'd worn Friday from the top of a pile on the end of my couch and walked quietly through the darkened kitchen into the bathroom to get some clean underwear and to change. Mom and Dad slept on; it was better they stay that way.

I was happy as we walked to our church up on the avenue and then sat with Jacky and his friends in the sanctuary balcony, where the older kids always sat. The junior and senior choirs marched solemnly down the center aisle, their voices leading the rest of us in the processional hymn. I knew many hymns. Back in fourth and fifth grades, I had been in the junior choir and had attended every week though I didn't have a good voice. Jacky and I had gone to church suppers, skits, and rummage sales, always without our parents. Once Jacky auctioned one of his model sailing ships that he had made by hand. Someone bought it for five dollars, which went to the church. Mom and Dad never noticed it was missing from the house.

Jacky played on the church basketball team and had several friends whose families attended regularly. Most of my friends were Catholic or Jewish, so without thinking much about it, I had gradually stopped going to church. But I was glad I'd come this morning. I liked the sanctuary, with its dark wood walls and stained glass windows, the pageantry of the service and its familiarity, saying the same things every time. Once in the junior choir, the minister's son, Mark, and I had fallen into hysterical laughter at the communion rail, disgracing ourselves. The minister ordered Mark not to hang around with me anymore. I escaped unpunished except for the memory, which picked at me and made me wonder whether I deserved to attend church. But everyone seemed to have forgotten it and Mark and his family had moved to another church.

After the service, we stood in line to shake hands with the new minister, Mr. Stevens, who had come the year before. He knew Jacky and welcomed him.

"Jack, wonderful to see you. Great game last week."

"Hello, Pastor John. This is my sister, May."

The minister, cheerful in his serious black robe, not like the old minister, shook my hand up and down.

"Welcome, May, welcome." His other hand gripped my arm. "I hope we see more of you. Please come and join our youth activities."

I wondered whether he thought he could shake me into returning and was glad when he let go of my hand. But I felt my face heat up when he looked into my eyes, making me remember the trips downtown to steal and the Hog River, and laughing at the communion rail.

We went to Maxwell's drugstore, all squeezed into one booth, and the older kids ordered coffee. I had a Coke. Jacky's best friend, Ron Michaels, who was very tall with curly blond hair and a friendly smile, talked with me the most. A girl with glasses and a nice pink sweater set named Jenny talked with me about the clothes the high school girls wore nowadays. Neckerchiefs were the big thing, and Jenny said she had lots and would give me one. But mostly they talked among themselves about kids I didn't know. After a while Jacky said quietly, "Why don't you go on home? We're going somewhere." None of them invited me to tag along.

I shrugged. "Okay. See you at home later?"

"Maybe not. I'm going to the bowling alley tonight."

I watched them leave and sat alone in the booth for a while with a true crime magazine, making my Coke last as long as I could. The library was closed. My money was gone. I'd have to go home. I'd retrieve the skirt first and wear it tomorrow. If Jacky asked, I'd say I borrowed it from Joanie. I'd make myself a tuna fish sandwich and Kool-Aid for supper tonight. Either that or chicken gravy and bread and save the tuna fish for sandwiches for Jacky and me to take to school. Maybe he'd make enough money from pin setting to lend me some.

*   *   *

With Joanie and Stella, I made another trip downtown and this time got a navy blue sweater and a white blouse to go with the gray skirt. Later, alone at Kamin's Five and Dime, I stole a bra to replace the one I had taken from Mrs. Shenk's clothesline. I also stole a pair of panties. That bra was so old it was gray and had ripped in several places. One day, I think it must have been in gym class as I changed as modestly as I could from my gym suit into school clothes, some girls caught a glimpse of my tattered bra.

Nothing was said at the time; that's why I'm not sure exactly when it happened. But soon some girls started making comments, calling me "DRB," at first not explaining it. Someone finally did: Dirty Ragged Bra. And they added "DBP," for Dirty Buggy Pants. I was mortified. I stopped being social, even skipped gym a couple of times, until I showed up wearing the brand new clean white bra and white panties, and the razzing died away. After that, for a long while, I avoided those girls in gym class and my homeroom.

*   *   *

The welfare check came at the beginning of the month. Dad sobered up, washed and shaved, dressed in a white shirt or one of his blue work shirt and dark trousers, black dress shoes, and an old black overcoat too big for him now. He walked to the bank on the corner of Albany and Blue Hills to cash the check and bought a month's supply of liquor and prescription drugs and a few groceries at nearby stores. The liquor store delivered to the door but I went with him to help carry the other packages. He gave me a dollar and turned the rest over to Mom in the belief, I guess, that she would buy more groceries. But the money stayed in her purse until Jacky or I retrieved it or Dad spent it for more liquor.

As far as I could tell, neither of my parents ever ate. Maybe they did while I was at school. I didn't give it much thought. I knew there wasn't enough for me and I was starting to hate chicken gravy and bread. I stole food from the Popular Market, slipping a large bag of pistachio nuts into a front pocket of my jeans and covering it with my blouse and jacket, but I never stole from the First National where Jacky worked.

I went to church with Jacky once more during this low period and again sat with him and the others in the balcony. It was Communion Sunday. I repeated the general confession, feeling like a liar because I knew I'd keep stealing, and took communion anyway.

CHAPTER 12

The Wine Bottle

One night in early spring, Jacky and I were asleep. Loud shouting and the sounds of fighting from the bedroom woke me up. I ignored it until Dad stumbled noisily through the kitchen into the living room and fell with a thud onto the bare floor in the middle of the room. He was groaning and mumbling. I rolled over to face the sounds but couldn't see him in the dark.

Jacky's voice was gruff. "Dad, go to sleep. We have to get up for school tomorrow." They both fell silent and I started to fall back asleep.

"Fucking bitch cut me." His faint, raspy voice and his Scottish accent made it sound like "fooking," less of a swear word to my ears. I always made sure to speak pure American, not to sound like them.

"Dad, we're trying to sleep!" I could hear Jacky getting up as he spoke. He switched on the overhead light.

"Oh, God, he's bleeding!"

I jumped up to look. Dad lay on his back on the bare wood floor. Blood ran steadily from a gash on his forehead down the side of his head into his fringe of hair. At first I saw only that.

"Look at his wrist."

"Oh, no."

His hand hung down, practically separated at the joint, pouring blood onto his pants, the floor, everywhere.

"She cut me with the wine bottle," Dad muttered, more bewildered than angry.

"Get a pan to catch the blood," Jacky said.

I rushed into the kitchen, a fury of adrenaline propelling me, and came back with the single towel I saw and an enamel bucket that long ago had soaked mops or diapers. Jacky pushed Dad's wrist and hand together, wrapped the towel around them, and propped it on the edge of the bucket so the wound more or less closed and the bucket caught the seeping blood. I got two more towels from the kitchen drawer, handed one to Jacky, and dabbed at Dad's forehead, feeling a pounding sense of dismay and panic.

Suddenly Mom barged into the room muttering and swaying from side to side. She pulled the blanket off my bed, turned and lunged toward her husband, knocking his wrist off the edge of the bucket with her foot, opening up the wound, which started pouring blood again. Jacky jumped up and shouted at her.

"Are you crazy? What are you trying to do, kill him?" He pushed her and she stumbled backward into the kitchen. He followed, pushing and pushing her toward the bedroom.

"Leave us alone, you drunken bitch!"

This shocked me. Jacky was the one who never showed his anger, wasn't home enough to attract much of Mom's wrath. She hadn't touched him since the time years before when she had whacked him on the bare back with a bamboo pole, drawing blood, and he had grabbed her arm and told her in a steely voice that he would hit her back if she ever hit him again.

I thought maybe Jacky didn't hate her as much as I did, that he wasn't under her control as much as I was. It crossed my mind now that maybe he did hate her.

I tried to prop Dad's wrist back on the bucket to stop the bleeding again. As I took hold of his arm, his worn blue work shirtsleeve opened and I saw a gaping slice all along his upper arm so deep it exposed something white. I fell backwards off my haunches, still holding my father's arm.

"Jacky! Look!"

He came back into the room.

"Jacky, we need help."

He bent down next to me. "Dad, Dad. Can you hear me?"

"What?" Dad looked sleepy.

"Your arm is cut too bad. We need to get an ambulance. You have to go to the hospital." Jacky pulled on his dungarees and engineer boots and put his jacket on over his tee shirt. "I'm going to the phone at the gas station. Get more towels to wrap around his arm."

He closed the door between the kitchen and the hallway to our parents' bedroom to discourage Mom from returning and went quickly out the door of the apartment. I could hear him jumping the stairs two at a time and wondered whether the neighbors heard too. It was still dark outside; normal people were sleeping. I got the towels from the kitchen closet and did what Jacky said. Daddy had a peaceful look on his face. His eyes closed, he breathed softly through his mouth. I thought he was awake but he didn't say anything or even grumble.

"Don't worry, Daddy. Jacky's gone for the ambulance. You'll be okay. The bleeding stopped." It hadn't really stopped. A red spot already showed on the last towel. It made me think of my period that I had gotten for the first time the previous Christmas Day. Was it only three months ago? But I had been pleased with that blood, which made me special. This, Daddy's blood, made me feel small and weak and angry. And it smelled of coming disaster.

It couldn't have been more than ten minutes before Jacky came back followed by two policemen. I knew they were coming when I saw flashing red lights chasing each other furiously around the walls and ceiling. Even so, my stomach lurched when I heard them at the door.

Jacky came in first. "The hospital wouldn't send an ambulance without the cops. They saw me running from the gas station and stopped me. I told them." He was trying to explain why he had brought strangers into our home, cops at that.

The cops called for an ambulance and more police. Before too long the ambulance came and took Dad to McCook, the public hospital. Jacky and one of the policemen went with them.

Another policeman, Frank, who regularly patrolled the neighborhood, spoke to me as the ambulance men carried the stretcher out. "How about you go in and tell your mother to get dressed to come downtown with us."

I looked at him like he was crazy, though his face was bland and his eyes were gentle as they tried to lock onto mine. "The wine bottle's still in there. She might stab me."

"No, she won't. She's finished for the night. She's probably already sorry." A slight smile played at one side of his mouth. "Anyway, we're here. Nothing more is going to happen." I wondered if he would tell the neighborhood foot patrolman, Tony, who all of us kids knew pretty well, what he had seen tonight.

I walked into the bedroom feeling as much shame and anger as fear. Mom actually looked sober.

"The cops want you to go with them."

"Why, what do they want?"

"They want to arrest you for almost killing Daddy." Spite surged through me as I said it, though my eyes wandered the dingy room, refusing to fix on my mother. I forced them to look into her face, which showed something new, fear. "I wish you were the one dead." I walked out of the room, ignoring her calling after me, "Me…." I went to the living room while the cops waited in the kitchen. I could hear them talking but couldn't hear the words; I didn't want to hear them.

Within minutes Mom came out of the bedroom in a white dress with blue flowers that I recognized from an earlier time. It hung loosely on her. Neither of us said anything.

And the cops said, "Let's go downtown so you can answer some questions."

After they left, I tried to clean the blood off the living room floor using dirty towels and a sheet from the overflowing hamper. I filled the laundry tub in the kitchen with water, soap, and bleach to soak all the bloody cloths. I sat in my mother's chair in the kitchen and smoked one of her cigarettes. It grew cold as the dawn came but I didn't move. Over and over in the silence my brain repeated, I wish she was dead, I wish she was dead, I wish she was dead.

Jacky came home from the hospital as I was getting dressed for school. He looked exhausted.

"They sewed up Daddy's wrist and arm and forehead. They had to put wires in his wrist to hold it together."

"The cops arrested Mom and took her to jail."

Before he changed for school, Jacky filled the kerosene can for the stove so we wouldn't have to do it that night.

School dragged. I relived the night's events, dwelling on how out of control things were, how little I, or even Jacky, could do about any of it.

After school, I hung around the apartment, without energy to look for my school friends or go to the library. I read the only things in the house, a children's book of bedtime stories and a pile of old *Upper Rooms*. I tried to straighten things up as best I could. I swept and washed the floors and added clean water and bleach to the still bloody towels and sheet. I hated putting my arm into the red water to pull the plug on my father's blood.

The next day as I played cards with a group of kids in front of the apartment building, I saw my mother walking down the street like a normal person. She had on the same flowered dress and wore her hair in a neat bun. She was sober. She stopped at the group, smiled, said hello to all of us, and put her hand on my shoulder. The other kids made like nothing had happened.

"Shall we go upstairs?"

I was speechless. The cop cars and ambulance had woken up the whole neighborhood and it had been in the newspaper this very morning that a woman had been arrested for attacking her husband with a wine bottle. It said her name and everything. How come they didn't keep her in jail? I got up and went into the building with her, away from the kids, who stared after us in silence.

We walked up to the second floor, Mom not saying anything. At the door to the apartment, I couldn't hold it in. "How could you? After what you did, just to come back here like everything's the same?"

I ran as fast as I could along the second-floor hallway and out onto the back porch. Mom didn't follow and I didn't hear her voice. I climbed over the railing, slid down the metal pole to the ground, and made my way to the back of the garage and through the window to the car. I lay down on the back seat and curled up as tight as I could get, breathing heavily although I had hardly been running at all. I wanted to cry but only two or three tears wet the corners of my eyes.

After dark I went back up to the apartment and found a note from my mother: I've gone to McCook to visit Daddy.

CHAPTER 13

Police Court

Spring came and the mass of mountain laurels on the church lawn bloomed all at once. Everyone tried to ignore what had happened. The neighbors stayed silent. Dad got out of the hospital after twenty-one days. He stayed drunk most of that time, on whiskey smuggled in by Mom. I visited in the early days but less often as it became clear nothing was going to change. Dad refused to press charges but the police put Mom on trial anyway. Both of them went to police court twice but the case was postponed.

The cop, Frank, still patrolled the neighborhood in his squad car, and every time he saw me he'd call me over and ask me how my mother was. Sometimes other kids were with me and it was embarrassing, so I'd just nod and walk away. Then Frank shot and killed a man who was running from him in a chase. It was a big scandal in all the newspapers, and he got a lot of criticism. The kids started shouting "Killer" at him as he drove around the avenue. Everybody hated him. One night he was in his car in front of the library. I approached him.

"Hey, Frank," I said, real quiet like I was telling him a secret, "how about you don't mention my problem and I won't mention yours? And I'll try to get the other kids to back off."

He nodded. "Okay."

He didn't say thank you, but he never asked about my mother again.

Months passed. Dad announced one Saturday morning that the judge wanted to see Jacky and me in court the next week.

"Why us? We didn't do anything!" said Jacky.

"I won't go. It's too embarrassing."

"You have to go. It's the law. And I want you to say this never happened before and won't happen again. That Mommy is sorry about what she did."

No one spoke until Jacky asked, "How do you know that, Dad?" I watched Jacky's expression as he looked at Mom, who sat in her black kitchen chair in front of the kitchen window. His face looked pinched and sad. Mom didn't say a word, but reached for her cigarette and took a long drag, not looking at any of us. She let the smoke out fast and immediately took another deep drag.

The night before the court appearance, both of them drank less than normal and went to bed early. In the morning they took baths, using the same water, a Scottish custom, and dressed in their best clothes. We all took the bus downtown, as if we were going on a family outing, like in the old days. We hadn't been out together like this since before Dad lost his job. It gave me a weird feeling, like we were going backward into history.

On the bus Dad tried to be jovial, and he nudged Mom once or twice in a friendly way, getting her to smile. I wished it were a Saturday morning and we were heading toward Dad's old job.

Jacky and I were the only kids in the crowded, noisy courtroom. Almost every space on the pew-like benches was taken. We had to squeeze into the middle of a row and ask people to shift down to accommodate us. From the close-packed smells, not everyone had taken baths that morning like our parents. We watched and listened for a while until the judge stopped the proceedings. He peered straight at me, and then at Jacky, whispered to a man in a uniform, and pointed to us.

"This case is not fit for the ears of children. You two, please wait outside until the bailiff calls you back."

The man in uniform came to get us. We had to get up and squeeze our way out of the narrow row while everyone stared. We waited in a noisy hallway with a sour smell of dirty mop water and stale cigarettes until the bailiff called to us to come back into the courtroom. Once we were in our seats, Mom's name was called out. As she stood and made her way toward the front of the room, she looked like a respectable woman. She had on a navy blue dress with a white collar and wore a white bead necklace and matching earrings. Dad had polished her white tie-up high-heel shoes for her that morning.

The judge was stern. "Mrs. Kilgour, you have two nice, well-behaved children to make a home for. Your husband has refused to press charges and I don't want to add to the turmoil your children have already been through. The charges are dismissed. I don't ever want to see you in my courtroom again."

I couldn't believe what the judge said. One part of me was glad. I thought Mom would be sent to jail or at least get probation. Another, larger, part of me was shocked, that the judge thought Mom could make a home for us, that he had used us as the reason to let her off. I darted out of the room ahead of the others.

"Where're you going, Me?" Dad called in his Scottish way.

I took the stairs two at a time past scruffy-looking people and uniformed policemen to get away. I walked home alone for an hour through a sunny afternoon that eventually slowed my pace and softened my mood. But as I walked and thought about my family, I knew the drinking and the ugliness would get worse. The previous night I had an awful dream, a nightmare. Mom was boiling in liquid gold in a big cauldron in the dark corner of the second floor hallway in front of the door of the Calloways who lived in 2C. She raised her hands to me pleading for help. I stood in the hallway transfixed. I couldn't move to help even if I wanted to. I woke with a fright about my mother's plight and my own indecision.

The nightmare remained vivid and would returned twice more in the next several weeks, but I wouldn't mention it to anyone. It wasn't right that my mother should be boiling in gold without rescue. But in my dream I never tried to help her.

CHAPTER 14

Summer

For eighth-grade graduation I wore a polka-dotted white dress and ballerina slippers that Jacky paid for. It was my first time wearing nylons. Jacky tried to earn enough for me to get my hair trimmed and curled in a permanent but rain cut into his weekend of caddying and there wasn't enough money. I didn't mind. I appreciated what he did. Without him, I would have had to skip graduation. It would have been impossible to steal a graduation dress and a pair of shoes.

Jacky attended the ceremony in the high school auditorium and waved to me when I caught his eye from my seat on the stage. Our parents didn't attend. They were back to staying drunk most of the time, as if the wine bottle incident hadn't happened. I was glad they weren't there, couldn't imagine them being there.

The day after graduation, I sat on the first floor back porch steps of our building reading a library book. Mr. and Mrs. Jones sat on the second-floor porch of their building. I could hear the low drone of Mr. Jones's voice as he read the newspaper to his blind wife. Then he called down to me.

"May, stay right there. We've got something for you."

Mr. Jones, in old black work pants and an undershirt, came down and went into their garage. He rolled Nancy's bike out and walked it to where I stood.

"Here," he said. "My wife tells me you'll be able to put this bike to good use. Nancy's gotten too old for it." He was a stout man with curly brownish red hair on his chest and shoulders. He smiled as I took the bike, too surprised at first to say anything.

"You got it?"

"Thank you…thank you, Mr. Jones. I…I don't know what to say." I was stuttering. I looked up toward the porch but didn't see Mrs. Jones.

"Don't say anything. Take it for a ride and see if it's to your liking. You'll be needing to put some more air in the tires."

I walked the bike down the driveway and along the street to Hy's gas station, topped off the air in the tires, and circled the block before pulling back into the yard. The bike clanked more than the Monarch and I'd have to buy batteries for the horn and light. But it fit me and would give me the wheels I needed for my travels. Mrs. Jones was back on their porch with her husband. I called up to them.

"Thank you, it's great! Please thank Nancy for me too!"

They waved and Mrs. Jones, in a dress with bright sunflowers on it that gave her a happy and carefree look, groped her way to the railing. "We're glad you can put it to use. Happy Graduation, dear."

I grinned and waved again. Then, remembering she couldn't see me, I called, "I'll take real good care of it, I promise."

I opened our garage door and squeezed the bike in between the car and the solid wooden wall between the garage and the garbage shed. My eyes had filled with tears and I had to stay in the garage long enough to dry them and rub my face back to normal. The Joneses had gone inside by the time I came out.

I got my book from the porch and went upstairs to the apartment, excited from such an unexpected gift. It had really been a pain to have no bike for almost two years.

The next morning I thought again about the kindness of the Joneses as I took my new bike out of the garage. They weren't just a good memory. They were good neighbors, friends, though my parents had long ago stopped being friendly in return. I rode the bike to the playground, planning to play paddle tennis with anyone I could find willing to play with me. I had gotten so good at paddle tennis I could usually beat the playground supervisors, grown men who taught school or coached the rest of the year. And I didn't think they let me beat them. I loved the rhythm of the game, the flow of running and hitting the ball, at the same time thinking ahead about my next move and my opponent's reaction.

I loved Keney Park, the broad sweep of grass that had once been a sheep farm, the shady playground, wooded trails and hidden glens, the pond house with its oiled wooden floor we could walk on in our skates in winter. Or at least I could until my skates got too small.

On this day, as on many others stretching ahead that summer, I met up with Stella and two of our new friends, Alex and Chip. We rode our bikes on the hard red clay roads in a circuit taking in Lookout Mountain, a steep hill used for sledding and tobogganing in the winter, and the more gentle Grandfather Hill where the little kids sledded.

At the top of Lookout Mountain, we went into our hideaway to smoke, a clearing surrounded by thick bushes and young trees that shielded us from anyone who might pass by. We talked about nothing in particular, lazing about on our backs under a green ceiling of low branches. I had paired off with Chip, whose real name was Lester. He was an ordinary-looking boy with brown hair cut in a butch and brown eyes. His smooth cheeks were often blotched red from bike riding or horsing around. I liked him well enough. Sometimes we kissed; sometimes we wrestled. He was just a little taller and heavier than I was. Chip's father was a fireman. Alex, whose father was a policeman, came from Maine and spoke with an accent. Stella and I didn't talk about our stealing because of Alex's father. The two boys lived on the other side of the park from us and would be going to a different school in the fall. The park was our main meeting place and summer days in the park were the limit of our dates.

The summer unfolded in some ways just as I wanted. Most mornings I rode my bike to Keney Park, played paddle tennis, softball, volleyball, or ring toss and hung out with Stella, Alex, Chip, Joanie, and other kids who came and went. Sometimes I stayed by myself reading. I read two or three books a week, keeping current with the library's new acquisitions rather than probing the shelves for good stories from earlier times. I read in the library, on the back porch in the sun, in the park, in the car on rainy days. I read true love and true crime magazines almost as often as I read the library books. I could read a whole magazine while nursing one Coke at Gourson's.

The trips downtown continued. Twice over the summer we saw the same security guard but he never caught us. Once when we saw him standing in the jewelry department, I had a bathing suit under my skirt and blouse. I badly needed that bathing suit, having outgrown the red one from my camp days. The other time we saw him in the misses' department before we had stolen anything, so we left empty-handed.

When I wasn't in the park, I rode my bike with my friends to more distant places like Mark Twain's House, Elizabeth Park for fishing and swimming, or Pope Park for swimming. On rainy days I went to the library or hung around the neighborhood, joining the kids my age and younger in their board games in the hallway or in someone else's apartment.

I slept at Joanie's house or in the garage a lot that summer to avoid the fights at home. At Joanie's I ate normal food, like canned spaghetti, sliced tomatoes, and hamburgers. To the garage I brought sodas, pistachio nuts, and potato chips and read until it got too dark. The alley was my toilet and skunk cabbage leaves my paper. In the morning, early, I went upstairs to wash and brush my teeth, trying hard not to wake my parents. Sometimes I didn't see them awake from one week to the next. If there were sounds of life in the apartment, I didn't go in. Instead, I rubbed the sleep from my eyes with my knuckles or used the restroom at the gas station to rinse my mouth and wash my face. I wore the same clothes until I could sneak into the apartment for long enough to wash something and then let it dry on the clotheslines strung from the back porch.

One muggy August morning around seven o'clock, I badly needed money. I went silently into my parents' bedroom on my hands and knees, heading for my mother's purse on the floor on the far side of the bed. A breeze had pulled the shades tight against the screens on the open windows and a musty yellow light bathed the room. The floor was sticky and smelled sour from spilt wine. The welfare check had arrived and been cashed the previous week but there was no decent food in the house. I opened the purse and took twenty dollars. The money was in my hand when my mother woke up.

"Thief! Stealing from your own family!"

That woke Dad up and he stumbled off the bed to block my escape. I jumped up, palming the money, and blocked his advance with my left arm. I ran into the kitchen and jumped over his chair, pulling the door to the living room shut behind me to gain time. I made it to the living room door, opened it, and ran halfway down the stairs before Dad reached the hall.

His deep voice shouted, "Don't come back! Stay in the street where you belong, like the whore you are!"

My insides cringed, knowing the neighbors, still home at that early hour, heard it all.

I kept running, out of the house, up the street, to the park. I ran as fast as I could all the way up Grandfather Hill. At the top, out of breath and sweating, I lay on my back on the thick wet grass and watched wispy clouds and birds move across the pale sky. Calming myself, I wondered what was going to happen next, feeling a mixture of shame and anger at myself as much as at my parents.

*   *   *

But nothing happened. I stayed out of the house completely, sleeping in the garage, which held the day's warmth through the night and allowed me to sleep uncovered, undisturbed. Jacky stayed out of the house more than I did, usually sleeping at the bowling alley. I learned that he too occasionally slept in the car when I found him curled up asleep in the backseat one night. That night I took the more cramped front seat.

CHAPTER 15

The Fall

By the end of that summer, tired of trying to figure out what to do with myself, I couldn't wait for school to start. I wanted to play basketball again and do the same orderly things every day.

I was in high school now and Weaver High was bigger than Jones, with a different teacher for each subject. I knew most of the kids in my homeroom. Mr. Bellamy, my teacher, wore bow ties, had frizzy red hair, and was friendly, goofy, and proper at the same time.

Three weeks after school started, a phone call came into my English class calling me to the dean of students' office. The other kids looked at me sideways, raising their eyebrows, snickering, but I couldn't think of anything I had done wrong, of any school rules I might have violated. I had a sinking feeling as I remembered the visit of the child abuse investigators. Were they going to do to me at Weaver what I had convinced them not to do to Jacky two years ago?

I walked to the main floor from my class in the basement. As I got to the wide hallway before the administrative offices, Sally Cox, who occasionally went downtown with Joanie and me to shoplift, passed close by going in the opposite direction.

"Deny it," Sally whispered. A woman followed behind her. A teacher? Her mother?

I felt my whole body tense up. This wasn't about child abuse. Should I run out the door, to the park, to the swings? I stood still in front of the office, thinking. The secretary looked up and motioned to me. I went to the window and gave her my name.

She frowned. "Sit over there."

I went where she pointed, in front of the dean of students' office. A sign on the closed door read: Barbara Baldwin, PhD. I sat for perhaps ten minutes, becoming calm and resigned to something bad happening, wishing I'd brought a book to escape into. I should never go anywhere without a book, I thought.

The door opened and Joanie and her mother walked out, both crying. Joanie looked at me and grimaced. Mrs. Dresser scowled, gripped Joanie's arm and hurried her along. I looked over Joanie's shoulder to see the dean motioning me into the office. The dean pointed to a chair in front of the desk. At the side of the desk sat someone I had never seen before. The dean, a motherly looking athletic woman with wavy gray hair and a tanned, lined face, took her seat behind the desk.

"Sit down, Miss Kilgour. This is Policewoman Pohanka."

Oh shit, went through my head. I sat and looked at the pretty blonde policewoman. She wore regular clothes, no uniform or gun. She stared into my eyes. I looked back and saw disapproval and suspicion. The woman held the stare like a cat claiming dominance. I looked away, toward the dean, at the wall, out the window where the green football field grabbed my gaze. That's where I wished I was, out there running around on the fresh-cut grass in the autumn air.

"Do you know why you're here?" The woman called me back inside the stuffy room.

"No."

"Well, I'll tell you then. We have evidence you've been shoplifting downtown. We've caught you and several others cold."

So that was it. I didn't feel any strong emotion like fear or anxiety. Instead, I felt empty. I looked at the floor in front of the desk, wondering what they expected me to say.

"Most of your gang confessed."

I looked up, "My gang?"

"Yes, you're one of the ringleaders. We know that."

"I'm not a ringleader. There's no gang." I paused, trying to think where she could have gotten that idea. "But I was the captain of the Cool Cats at Jones and of a softball team this summer." Their looks told me the joke wasn't appreciated.

"You think you're pretty smart, don't you? Well, you're not smart enough. Security officers at G. Fox and at Sage-Allen have been observing you. Others caught red-handed at the scene implicated you. We've been collecting evidence for several months."

I didn't say anything. A deep hole had opened in the middle of me.

"Do you deny it?"

I shrugged but stayed quiet. What was there to say?

"I want you to tell me with whom you shoplifted. I know about Joan Dresser, Stella Pagano, Judith Stein, Mary Ann Clark, Belinda Sullivan, Sally Cox, and Doris Bergman. Who else?"

The list surprised me. "I never went downtown with all those kids." Were all of us shoplifting without knowing about the others?

"Your parents are going to be brought into this, of course. What do you think they'll say?"

I shrugged again. "I don't know." The hollow spot inside echoed the words: I don't know, don't know, know, no, leave me alone.

Mrs. Baldwin spoke for the first time. "May, why did you steal? You know it's wrong, don't you?"

I looked at each of them in turn. My eyes came to rest on the policewoman. No point in denying it. They knew everything already.

"Yes, but I needed that stuff. It was mostly clothes." I didn't mention the food.

"That's no excuse." The policewoman stared at me again, with unwavering brown eyes, her mouth set in a downward curve like a fish. "You're pretty tough, aren't you? Nothing fazes you. You're not even upset at getting caught. You're not crying, pleading with us not to tell your parents."

I sat there staring straight ahead. Was I tough? I didn't think so. Suddenly an odd sensation came over me: The policewoman became very small, tiny and far away, as did Mrs. Baldwin, the furniture, the room itself, as if at the wrong end of a huge telescope. Had the other girls cried and pleaded? I couldn't seem to care. What did it matter? Emboldened for no reason I could explain, though it struck me as weird to speak to such tiny people in such a tiny room, I said in a voice that sounded as hard and flat as ice, "My parents have their own problems."

"Who else shoplifted with you?"

"No one." Flashes of light pulsated where the policewoman's face should have been. How strange. Was I going to faint, like my mother once had in Woolworth's downtown? I had never had such a weird sensation. I squeezed my eyes closed to stop the light, but it pulsed even worse, blazing white against black. I opened my eyes again and looked at both women.

The policewoman leaned back in her chair as if finished. She took out a folder and started writing in it. She handed some papers to Mrs. Baldwin and continued writing. Mrs. Baldwin read the few pages, took a pen from a holder on the desk, signed the last page, and handed them back to the policewoman. I could see everything except what I focused on. From the side I sensed Mrs. Baldwin gazing at me, so I looked out at the football field again. The single sound in the room was the scratch of a pen on paper followed by rustling and more scratching. I was the subject of all this scratching yet I wouldn't get to read it.

The policewoman spoke. "Your case is being referred to the Juvenile Court. You're to report to Mrs. Smart at her office in Juvenile Hall tomorrow afternoon at 3:15. She'll be your investigating officer. You're to bring to her office all of the merchandise you've stolen. Take this letter home to your parents. Bring the signed copy with you tomorrow."

I stood to take the envelope and remained standing. The room returned to normal size and the flashing light disappeared. Both women stood and looked at me. I wondered if the strange sensations were visible on my face. Mrs. Baldwin's face was sad. Miss Pohanka's face showed annoyance, maybe resignation, but no sympathy.

"Should I go back to my class?" Mrs. Baldwin nodded, handing me a pass. I walked out of the room feeling normal again and, with it, came a huge sense of relief. I could have been taken that very day to the Detention Center, as Mom had been taken to jail the night of her crime.

The clock in the hallway showed, amazingly, that less than fifteen minutes had passed. Stella sat in the outer office looking scared and gave me a weak smile. I felt something like an ache passing between us. Stella's father came from Italy and was strict.

As I walked back to English class I read the letter. It informed my parents by name that I had been caught shoplifting and was being ordered to appear before Juvenile Court authorities for further investigation. The letter instructed them to contact Mrs. Catherine Smart as soon as possible. It was typed, not what the policewoman had been writing on. At the bottom was a space for my parents to sign that they had received, read, and understood the letter.

I drooped. My mother and father would have to surface before the authorities again. What would happen if they didn't? Or if they showed up drunk at the Juvenile Court? Or if the cops came and found them drunk? What would they do?

What would Jacky think? He worked so much he didn't have time for trouble. Or, unlike me, he was just naturally good.

Reaching my English class as the bell rang, I joined the throng of kids in the hallway and took the stairs to my next class, looking for familiar faces. Mary Ann and Doris were whispering together as they headed to the third floor. When I approached, they stopped talking.

"We'd better not be seen talking together. It'll be worse," Doris said.

"How could it be worse?" I asked. "They've already caught us."

"Yeah, but they think we're in some kind of gang. And we're not. I hardly know you."

We went in different directions as we reached the third floor. There was something in her voice. Was I being branded as the ringleader, the one being blamed the most?

When I got home that afternoon, Mom and Dad were both drunk but awake.

"Guess what. I got caught shoplifting. Here's a letter for you to sign." I put the letter on the kitchen table, closer to Dad than to Mom.

Dad fumbled around looking for his glasses until he found them on his forehead, making me smile. He read the letter out loud. When he finished, he pushed his glasses back onto his forehead. Mom lifted herself slowly from her black chair to get her own look at the letter.

"Goddamn it," said Dad, moving his head from side to side in slow motion.

"You've disgraced us," Mom said after she read the letter.

"I've disgraced you? Wow, that's a switch!"

"Watch your tongue. That's no way to speak to your mother."

I had fallen into a hole like Alice in Wonderland, thrust back to early childhood when my parents expected obedience. "Well, I'm sorry about that," I said. "Maybe if you gave me money for school clothes I wouldn't steal them!"

As I often did to get away from them, I walked out and went to the garage by an indirect route in case they came after me. I didn't care what they thought, but my teeth clenched as I thought about Jacky and the neighbors finding out. The other kids would probably be told to stop hanging around with me. Maybe my school friends, the ones with respectable parents, would shun me. Joanie's attic refuge would be gone.

I stayed in the garage until late, reading and playing solitaire. I had put cardboard over the small windows in the garage door, which blocked the light from my flashlight, preventing anyone from knowing I was there. When I went back up to the apartment Mom and Dad were asleep. I ate bread soaked with condensed milk and went into the living room to my bed. Jacky turned over in his bed.

"You're up shit creek now, kiddo."

"It's not funny, Jacky." I made a face at him in the dark.

"It's an expression. But you are in trouble this time. You know that, don't you?"

"Yeah, I know. But what else was I supposed to do? I had to have clothes for school."

"You don't need to explain it to me. But the cops aren't going to care about that. And Mom and Dad aren't going to make a good impression on anyone."

"That's for sure." I fell into a fitful sleep, wary that my mother might retaliate by a punch or hair pulling in the night.

CHAPTER 16

Disgrace

The next day I walked to school looking for differences in the way people treated me. My classes, general business, civics, English, and algebra, went on forever, my mind unconnected from all of it. I learned in bits and pieces from the others that they all had appointments at different times at Juvenile Hall.

"My parents restricted me for life. I'm not going to be able to do anything except go to school, and they're talking about transferring me to Catholic school," said Stella.

"I've been ordered to stay away from all the other thieves." Doris Bergman smiled nervously as she said the word.

Joanie said, "Yeah, well, my mother is saying she's going to get tougher on me and make me find new friends. She even suggested we move out of state!"

I didn't say anything, glad I didn't have respectable parents to hurt. Anyway, stealing wasn't as bad as cutting someone open with a wine bottle.

After school, I filled two paper grocery bags with about half of what I'd stolen over the past year. I couldn't return all of it or I'd have nothing to wear except my graduation dress. I carried the bags, one in each arm, to the corner and took the bus to Washington Street. It took a transfer to get there, and I arrived at Juvenile Hall at exactly 3:15.

It was a looming old mansion of large, dirty, brick-colored stones, on a street mostly of stately government buildings. Tall maple trees, with leaves already drying to the colors of fall, dotted the wide lawn. My heart beat so loudly I could hear it as I walked up the steps to the porch. Through the glass in the front door I could see a small reception area. Pushing the heavy door open, I went into a room that was hot and smelled of ink and machines. I waited for the lady typing at the desk to look up. When she did, I gulped and tried to smile but my lips stuck to my teeth. The lady looked irritated by the interruption.

"I'm supposed to be here at 3:15, to see Mrs. Smart."

"Kilgour?"

"Yes." I put the two bags on the desk.

The lady pushed a clipboard across the desk toward me and pointed to a room to her right. "Take a seat in there and fill out this form." She put my two bags of good school clothes on the other side of the desk on the floor and returned to the papers on her desk.

I watched my clothes move away forever, took the clipboard and a pen and went in the direction the lady had pointed. What would they do with my clothes? Would they put them to better use than I had?

A black man and woman with a boy sat on one side of the waiting room and a white woman and boy sat across from them. I smiled at each of the groups in turn but they looked back at me with blank faces. I sat in a ratty upholstered chair against the far wall and started filling out the form. It was long and wanted to know all about me. The usual, like my address, school, grade, age, parents' names, but also questions about my health history, grades, psychological testing. They wanted to know my parents' jobs, ages, and court records. I left a lot of it blank. What did I know about health, except that Jacky and I had both had measles and chicken-pox, that I had peritonitis once, that Dad had heart trouble, and that Mom once broke her arm carrying Jacky's bike up to the second floor. And that Jacky's mumps had saved us from the circus fire. At the bottom I was supposed to sign, and it had a space for parents to sign also. Should my parents have come with me today?

Filling out the form with my best penmanship slowed my heart's pounding. When I finished what I could, I peeked at the other people in the room but their eyes avoided mine. The black boy finally looked at me, raised his eyebrows and opened his eyes wide, as if to say, "Look what we got ourselves into." His face straightened itself when his father glared at him.

A picture on the wall showed a beach scene with sailboats in the water and wispy clouds spread across the sky. The beach sand was finely detailed, as if the artist had set his easel right there and focused on it, stretching out finally to the less important distant scene. It made me remember my search of the Wadsworth Athenaeum for a painting of fruit at the beach by Salvador Dali. If that picture had looked like this one, I would have found it in a flash. Mr. Perkins, the student teacher in eighth-grade English, had assigned us to study the picture, which had a long title that I couldn't remember, and write an essay about what it meant. A bunch of us kids had wandered the museum looking for the picture and ended up going all the way back to the entrance to ask the attendant where it was. We had passed right by it. It was totally weird and disembodied, sinister somehow, although the colors were clean and bright. I'd written in my essay that the artist was playing with the viewer and I hadn't appreciated the undescriptive title he had given what was basically a hodgepodge of objects and scenes on a sheet of sand and sky. I was also annoyed at having wasted an hour looking for it, although normally I loved the Wadsworth Athenaeum, but I didn't mention that in my essay. Usually I got As and B-pluses in English except for pure grammar, but Mr. Perkins gave me a B, and wrote on my paper that the painting deserved more introspection than I had given it. I looked up the word in the dictionary. I didn't think Dali spoke to anything inside me. I couldn't relate to the jumbled painting, from the partial head of a man, another of a dog, and a scene from an African village together with a piece of rope and a fish made out of sky. I was all one piece for sure, and liked paintings that were too. Though I had to admit the world around me – Mom and Dad, school, and now this shoplifting charge – sure seemed disconnected.

The lady at the desk called the families away one at a time until I was alone. I thought about the other kids, the ones in my "gang." Had they already come and gone? I looked at my Mickey Mouse watch, Jacky's birthday gift. Was it only ten days ago? It seemed longer ago than that. I felt older than fourteen. When I reminded my parents that it was my birthday, Mom said it would have to wait for the next month's check. Yeah, sure.

Already four o'clock; my mind slipped into a daydream. In dappled sunlight on Pinetree Hill in Keney Park, I lay with my head against a tree trunk, having just buried a valuable prize at the base of the tree and covered the spot with a thick bed of pine needles. Someday when I was grown and far away from here, I'd come back and retrieve it. I opened a thick book with a colorful paper jacket and chewed on a penny stick of black licorice. Four more sticks lay in a row across my chest.

"Okay, come with me." The desk lady beckoned me, knocking the book, the scene, the scent of pine right out of my head. I got up and followed her through the reception area into a narrow, brightly lit corridor. The lady stopped at an open door and pointed me into a small, crowded room. Another woman who didn't smile sat at a small desk. She was big and rough looking, like a farmer's wife might be, except that she wore glasses and had on a gray dress with black flowers on it. Piles of paper and folders covered the desk. That was what made the desk small: It was buried under paper.

"I'm Mrs. Smart. Take a seat. Where's your form? Where are your parents?"

I sat on a wooden chair at the side of the desk and handed over the whole clipboard. "I didn't know they were supposed to come. No one said anything."

"All right. An investigator will visit them at your home."

Damn.

Mrs. Smart read the whole form, making notes on a separate piece of paper. She put it and the form I had filled out in a folder along with other papers she also read slowly. Several minutes passed in silence during which I studied her out of the corner of my eye, wondering whether she was smart like her name, glad my own nose was not as long and pointed. I looked around the crowded room; it seemed put together from rummage sale furniture and lamps. There were no curtains on the window and the floor was covered with a faded rug.

"I see that you're called May."

"Yes."

"Okay, May, here's how it'll work. You admit you shoplifted, correct?"

"Yes." What if I'd said no?

"We'll look into your records at school, evaluate your home life, send you for tests, and prepare a report for the juvenile court judge. This will all take several weeks. And you're to have no contact with your shoplifting companions."

I smiled at the expression.

Mrs. Smart stared at me, a surprised look on her face. "Do you think this is funny?"

"Not exactly."

"You're in serious trouble. We don't take shoplifting lightly here. Do you understand that?"

"Yes. I just don't think of them that way, as shoplifting companions. There isn't a gang, honest." I tried smiling again but this lady wanted none of it. Mrs. Smart looked back at her notes and wrote for several minutes. Was she writing that I wasn't taking any of this seriously enough?

"You're to report to me every week on this day, same time. I'll be watching you closely. I expect you to keep your nose clean and stay away from your so-called friends. Is that clear?"

I nodded, not moving my mouth in case a smile or a wisecrack came out by mistake.

The woman handed me two letters, one addressed to my parents, the other to the Board of Education, Department of Testing.

"This letter informs your parents that an investigator will be visiting them sometime next week. This one you take with you next Monday to the address indicated. They'll give you the tests we need for our investigation. The time is marked on the envelope. Any questions?"

I looked out the window. Through the heavy mesh screen I could see it was already almost dark. I felt weary, wondered where I was going to find the bus fare to come here every week without stealing it. I wanted to mention that to Mrs. Smart, explain that I wasn't really a bad girl. But all I said was, "No."

"I'll see you next week, then. Stay out of trouble, you hear me? If you have any questions you can call me. Here's my number."

Released from those suspicious eyes and the stifling room, I pocketed her card and left without answering, through an empty front hall, and out the door.

The street was busy with traffic. I unbuttoned my sweater and walked fast along the sidewalk, past people leaving their offices to go home, to their families, to dinner. No one paid any attention to me. I slowed my pace to look for a bus stop, stopped at the first one I came to, and waited for the bus to take me home, to my family, my dinner, whatever it would be. I had to stand the whole way.

Mom and Dad listened to my account of the session with Mrs. Smart and didn't say much except to berate me for shaming them.

"It's good our family isn't nearby to hear about this," Mom muttered. I didn't bother to answer, just watched her take a drag on her cigarette and reach for her glass of port wine, which they now drank because it was cheaper than whiskey.

"An investigator will be visiting you here next week, time unannounced. Here's the letter." I handed it to Mom with a mean look. "You might want to try not to get too drunk until after he's gone."

Dad said, "Don't be lecturing us, lass. There's no need to disrespect your mother over this."

Jacky wasn't there to comfort me or chew me out for making it worse.

CHAPTER 17

Waiting

I tried to follow all the rules, answering their questions about the color of apples and the meaning of inkblots, taking two buses every week to make my appointment at Juvenile Hall. Mrs. Smart sometimes kept me five minutes, sometimes thirty, probing for information, connections, reactions. I told her as little as possible, especially about my home life, the area she probed the most. It was too embarrassing and I resented her knowing this personal stuff.

When the sessions ended, I took the bus home through heavy traffic, half my brain observing the other passengers, the other half daydreaming. I imagined myself falling in love on a winter afternoon while skating at the Keney Park pond, a tall, handsome boy looking at me while he skated backward, pulling me along. Suddenly the brown water of the Hog River or Bobby's face would drive the daydream away. Or it would be the hiss of the brakes or the jolt of another passenger.

Life was boring: school, home, Juvenile Hall, waiting. Weaver had no afterschool sports for girls. I missed that a lot until I found a program at the recreation center up Blue Hills Avenue near the Bloomfield border, which was open for girls from six to nine o'clock two nights a week. I waited for the investigation to be finished. Mrs. Smart wouldn't tell me how much longer it would take. Jacky had to go for an interview. When he came home, he was somber.

"I don't know, May, it doesn't look good."

"What doesn't?"

"That lady kept asking about parental guidance, were you getting any."

"What'd you say?"

"I told her you had always been doing okay except for the shoplifting and you had stopped that."

"What'd she say?"

"Nothing. I had the feeling she didn't believe me."

I became wary of Mrs. Smart's power. Where was this leading? I asked her but she just frowned. The other gang members went their separate ways. Stella transferred to Catholic school, prohibited from seeing or telephoning any of her old friends. At school, we passed in the halls but avoided other contact in case anyone was watching. I met Joanie and the others by chance at the library or at the night basketball program at the recreation center, but Joanie seemed to lose her interest in sports, so I saw her less and less. One night at the rec center after a pick-up game, one of the girls, Mary Ann Clark, who I hadn't realized was a shoplifter, caught up with me as we left the building.

"Hey, May, what do you think about what's going to happen to you?"

"What do you mean?"

"I heard you were going to reform school, to Long Lane. Because of your home life. That's what my probation officer said."

My sweat chilled as we walked down the sidewalk to the street. I needed time to think. "Your case already went to court? You're on probation already?"

Mary Ann nodded. "Last week. I got a year's probation. Sally and Doris got a year and Stella got six months. She transferred schools, you know. Joanie got a year, but I heard she and her mother are moving to Hollywood. In Florida, not California."

"Really? I know about Stella, but I hadn't heard about Joanie moving."

"She told me about it when I saw her down at Juvenile Court."

"What else did you hear about me?"

"That's it. Because of your parents, you can't keep living at home." Mary Ann stopped walking and put her hand on my arm to stop me. "Hey, I thought you already knew."

Though in the shadows between two streetlamps, I struggled to keep my face unchanged. "Yeah, just checking. It's not completely certain yet. See you tomorrow." We walked in opposite directions.

How could they tell someone else before telling me? How could they give me a worse punishment because of my parents? I walked fast along the dark sidewalk, started running, trying to beat the anger out through the soles of my sneakers. I passed comfortable homes in the neighborhood just west of Blue Hills. It was about nine o'clock and most of the houses were still brightly lit. I could see people sitting together in living rooms and dining rooms. Some sat on front porches, enjoying the still pleasant crisp October evening. No one noticed me.

I was home in half an hour. Jacky wasn't there. My parents were both dead to the world. I made a tuna fish sandwich and drank a glass of water from the tap.

Should I run away? Maybe Jacky could lend me some money. Where would I go? New York was too scary. What could I do? Could I pass for sixteen and get a job? I had just turned fourteen but could probably pass for fifteen, maybe sixteen. But they'd ask for a birth certificate, wouldn't they?

I undressed and curled up under the blanket, hugging my knees to my chest. I tried to stay awake for Jacky to come home, but couldn't. He wasn't there in the morning, which meant he had stayed at the alley all night. Or maybe he was in the garage.

I waited the two days until my next appointment with Mrs. Smart. The time passed so slowly I felt I was back in the world of tiny people inside a telescope, the sensation I'd had that day in the dean's office and a couple of times since. When Thursday came, I practiced my arguments as I rode the bus. Yes, I knew shoplifting was against the law. I knew I had done wrong. But what about justice? How could I be punished worse for committing the same crime as the other kids? Wasn't that illegal? And didn't I at least have a better excuse for stealing, compared to the kids from better-off homes?

I walked up the stone steps of the gloomy mansion, for the first time noticing how the stone was worn in the middle of each step. Kids carrying their sad stories into this place had done that. By now I knew the detention center was on the second floor and the rear of the first floor. I had seen the heavy metal locked doors separating those parts of the building and caught glimpses of the kids on the other side. They looked like regular kids, no different from me.

To the right was a door leading into the wood-paneled offices of the judge. I went to the left as usual, down the narrow corridor lined with bulletin boards and radiators to Mrs. Smart's hot, cramped office. I knocked twice on the closed door and waited, my mouth as dry as an ink blotter. I wiped my palms on the sides of my jacket.

"Come in." Mrs. Smart's voice sounded weary. I opened the door and went in. Without looking up from the stacks of paper in front of her, Mrs. Smart said, "Sit."

I sat in the worn wooden side chair.

"Tell me about your activities this week." Weariness showed on her face, too, and I knew I contributed to it. She turned her swivel chair toward me and tucked a few strands of bristly gray hair behind her ears. She peered at me over glasses perched halfway down her nose, a nose too thin for her broad face. Or glasses too heavy from all her microscopic reading of police reports and school records and sad stories.

I listed all the good things I could think of: errands for people in the neighborhood, the five dollars my aunt had sent, a belated birthday present, Bs on two tests, playing in two winning basketball games at the rec center. Mrs. Smart asked me questions: which neighbors, which aunt, which subjects were the tests in, who else was on my basketball team. She wrote without looking at me. Finally, I fell silent and waited for her to talk about my future. But she said nothing, just sat writing notes with wrinkled, freckled hands as she did at the end of every session, leafing back and forth through my file as she wrote.

I couldn't walk out of that room without knowing. I couldn't stand the uncertainty for another week. "Mrs. Smart, I heard something from one of the other girls that bothered me."

Mrs. Smart looked up from her writing. "Yes?"

"She said all the girls except me were getting probation. But I was getting sent up—to Long Lane."

"Who said that?"

"One of the kids I played basketball with. I won't tell you her name."

"She spoke out of turn. The judge is the one who makes such decisions."

"But will your report make that recommendation?"

Mrs. Smart looked at the folder, then straight at me with an expression on her face I couldn't read. "The investigation isn't complete yet. And it's not my report. Many people contribute to it. My job is to pull it all together. I'm still waiting for information on your school records." She stopped talking and peered over the top of her glasses at me, making me shrink further into the straight wooden chair, waiting for the bad news hiding in the droop of her mouth, the slight twitch of her nose.

She went on, "But May, your parents don't provide an adequate home for you. They haven't made any effort to contact me, either on the phone or by coming here. When the investigator went to your apartment, twice, he found indications your parents had been drinking and the apartment was disheveled and dirty. It's all written in his report. They give you no supervision. You run wild." Her voice became softer, almost kindly, like Mrs. Floyd's voice at the library. "The neighbors and your teachers confirm that. Even your parents report that you don't obey them."

"I don't run any wilder than the other kids." I could feel the anger in my voice and tried to keep it under control. "And I didn't do anything worse than they did. How can my punishment be worse?"

"But if you are sent to Long Lane it won't be to punish you. It will be to give you a better environment."

"A better environment? In a reform school? Locked up? You think that's better?" My voice rose against my will. I was close to crying and laughing at the same time.

"Yes, May. You need discipline, three meals a day, and a clean bed to sleep in. There's a school on the premises as well as a good recreation program."

"What about equal punishment for equal crime?"

Mrs. Smart smiled, then tried to hide it. "I think you're incorrectly quoting someone. Juvenile justice always tries to take the child's background into account."

Anger and a feeling of helplessness welled up inside me. "But it's not fair!"

Mrs. Smart's voice took on a firmer tone. "That's for the judge to decide."

Against all of my strongest efforts, I started crying. Mrs. Smart handed me a box of tissues and went back to writing.

"You can go when you're ready, dear."

I went, my question answered, my future sealed.

CHAPTER 18

Alternative Futures

Now all I had to do was wait for the court hearing, which was even harder now that I knew what was going to happen. Mrs. Smart said to expect it within the month. I asked Jacky whether I should run away and he advised against it. He had done it several times and had always come home after two or three weeks, and he was a boy better able to live on the streets. It was already November and turning cold.

I kept going to school, slept at home most nights, other nights in the garage, burrowing under the newspapers for warmth from the autumn chill. My mother left me alone these days and stayed mostly in the bedroom with the door closed. Dad continued to fall asleep sitting in the kitchen most nights. Jacky came home late after working at the market and going directly from there to his pin-setting job. Or he didn't come home at all. One night he skipped the pin setting and was already home when I arrived about nine o'clock. He sat in Dad's chair in the living room reading, which was unusual for him.

"Guess what, May. I'm joining the Navy right after graduation. Dad signed the papers tonight." He waved a handful of pamphlets that he'd been reading.

My heart sank, though he had talked about it as a dream for at least a year. His entire face glowed with the excitement of the dream coming true, changing it, especially his eyes, which seemed deeper and brighter. I covered up my sadness or maybe it was fear. "That's great, Jacky. Is Ron going too?" He was Jacky's best friend.

"Ron, and a whole bunch of other guys. It's called the Kiddy Cruise. If you go in before the age of eighteen, you get out just before your twenty-first birthday. I'll be in for three years." He lit two cigarettes and handed one to me.

"Well, I'll be in Long Lane by then. You won't have to worry about me."

The happiness left his face. "I'll worry about you but maybe less with you there than if you stayed here. You know what I mean?" He had been stretched out in Dad's chair in the living room, his legs dangling over one of the arms, but he brought his feet to the floor and sat up straight. "Maybe it won't be so bad."

I sat on my half of the couch, back to the wall. "Yeah, it's a great place. You know they call it Wrong Lane, don't you, instead of Long Lane? You can learn all you need to know to get into the Niantic women's prison. The fast lane to a ruined life."

"You don't need to go that way, May. Mrs. Smart said plenty of the girls who come out of Long Lane at eighteen go on to good jobs, even to college."

"Since when are you on Mrs. Smart's side?"

"I'm not on her side. I'm on your side. But we both need to leave this place, get away from Mom and Dad. They're only going to get worse, you know that."

I felt morose and alone. June was only seven months away.

"Maybe you could join the Navy after you graduate. They take girls, you know."

"They do?" I thought about that for a minute. "Well, I'm thinking of quitting school at sixteen so I can work."

"That'd be dumb. Especially if you're still in Long Lane."

I had forgotten that. I changed the subject. "Do you hate them as much as I do, Jacky?"

"Yeah. Maybe more. I hate him especially," he whispered, pointing toward Dad in the kitchen, his head slumped forward in awkward oblivion. "He's a total failure." His voice had become hard, with a bit of meanness in it.

"At least Dad isn't violent, Jacky, like Mom is. That's what I hate the most about her."

"But Dad started it all. He was the one who was always drunk, even way back. In those days, she hardly drank at all. Maybe you don't remember. Besides, Dad is the man. He's supposed to provide for his family, and he doesn't. And he didn't before the heart trouble either."

"Yeah. Without you, I'd have to steal all my food, too. I probably would've gotten sent to Long Lane long before now!" As true as this was, I said it with a joking voice that made him smile. "You know, Jacky, when we're grown I'm going to pay you back all the nickels and dimes and dollars you've lent me."

He smiled again. "You'd better!"

Dad began stirring. Jacky got up and closed the door to the kitchen. He sat again, this time on the cushions he used as a bed, lost in thought, and didn't say anything for a couple of minutes.

Finally, he said, "I don't know why Dad became such a drunk. I think it might have to do with his family back in Scotland. You know, his father disowned him when he came to the States."

"I didn't know that. How come?"

"Because Dad was the only son and namesake. His father wanted Dad to stay in Scotland. Mom told me once. Our grandfather wouldn't allow Dad's sisters to write to him, and refused to read his letters. That's why we never had any contact with his side of the family."

"What does that have to do with his drinking?"

"I don't know. You knew he was married to someone else before Mom who died in childbirth and that we have a half-brother, didn't you?"

"I knew that, and his grandparents adopted the baby and changed his name, and then they wouldn't let Dad even see him. And Dad never talks about it. Do you think that caused him to drink?"

"Could be. Maybe he was angry and started drinking out of spite, or guilt, or loneliness. Whatever. Now he's just a drunk."

*   *   *

For the next several days I moped my way through life, trying to hide my sadness from Jacky, whose mood stayed buoyed by his decision to join the Navy. I tried to imagine going to court and being sent to Long Lane. Reading true crime magazines wasn't much help. They focused more on the crime than on the punishment. I imagined long lines of faceless girls wearing the same color of loose dress, brown or another ugly color, without belts so they couldn't hang themselves. They wore sneakers with no laces that flopped as they shuffled along windowless corridors. I saw myself sitting in a class of dunces learning nothing, or sleeping on a canvas cot in a room like an army barracks with bars on the windows. The walls of thick stone glistened from dampness. I would have to make friends with tough, criminal girls not like myself, unless the normal-looking kids at Juvenile Hall had ended up at Long Lane. Wrong Lane. Boring Lane. Dead End Lane.

CHAPTER 19

Mom

One night in early November, just a few days after my mother's uncelebrated fiftieth birthday, Jacky and I came home at about the same time. Dad was awake and waiting for us, dressed as if going to cash the welfare check.

"I think your mother is sick. She hasn't moved all day. I called Dr. Felder but he wouldn't come."

We went to peer at our mother from the bedroom door. Jacky went in and touched her forehead with the back of his hand, like Mom herself used to do to us.

"She's hot."

Dad nodded. "She has a high fever," he said. "I think she needs to be in a hospital. I'm going to the gas station to make the call."

The ambulance came and took her to McCook. Dad went with them, looking sober in his check-cashing clothes. I made supper of scrambled eggs and hamburger for Jacky and me.

The next morning we skipped school to wait for him. He didn't come home until midmorning.

"Your mother has pneumonia. We should have brought her in much earlier, they told me."

"How long will she be in the hospital?" I asked.

"I don't know, but I want you kids to visit her as much as you can."

The next day and practically every day for more than a week we went to the hospital. We almost never went together. Dad went during the day. I went after school. Jacky squeezed it in when he could.

I walked to McCook along Ridgefield Street with its beautiful houses bordering Keney Park. It took thirty minutes but was a pleasant walk and shorter than taking two buses. I wondered what it would be like to live in such a house. I knew one boy from school who lived on Ridgefield. He was tall and handsome, never fooled around or got into trouble, and was friendly to everyone.

If I lived in such a house my father would have to have a good job. Maybe Mom would work too, while Jacky and I went to school. I'd have my own room and so would Jacky. Mine would look out on the park so I could see trees all the time. The kitchen would be big and clean and warm. The oven would have cookies in it. My mother would lay out cookies and milk for me and my friends and ask us how our day had gone. I knew kids who lived like that.

At the end of Ridgefield, at the school for the blind, I had to go down a steep hill to reach the hospital, and up it on the return walk. I could have walked through Keney Park if it had been warmer and the days longer.

I went into the hospital through the main door and walked up to the second floor. My mother was in a room by herself, in a narrow hospital bed with an oxygen tent over it. Sometimes she was covered with a blanket to her neck. Other times, her arms lay on top of the blanket. But the oxygen tent separated her.

There was no chair in the room. I stood at the side of the bed for a time watching to see if she moved. I tried to talk with her.

"Mom, do you hear me? It's May. It's your daughter, Mary Cameron." My middle name was the same as my mother's, my grandmother's maiden name. That was a Scottish custom. I thought it might help Mom hear me.

There never was any answer. Over several visits I made other attempts. I pressed against the plastic until I reached Mom's thin soft arm or leg. I tapped gently, "Mom, wake up. Wake up." Another time I said, "Will you wake up if I tell you I love you?" She didn't. She slept on and on, as if tired of life. Her expression was peaceful but her face was almost the color of the sheet.

After a while I sat on the floor, leaning against the wall, stretching my legs across the clean, polished wood. My faded blue Keds pointed toward the ceiling. The room was rather large for just one bed. I looked at my mother's flat body in the center of the room inside the tent, lit by a strong ceiling light that reflected off the plastic, wondering what was going to happen next. I couldn't be angry with her while she was sick. I couldn't blame her for anything, though I thought I should.

One evening while I stood at my mother's bedside, a nurse came in to check the oxygen tank. She looked at me as she turned to go.

"Your mother is very sick, you know."

"Yes."

"She's in a coma."

I nodded but I didn't say anything, though I wasn't sure what a coma was.

"She's very, very sick." Then she left. She was the only person who talked to me in the whole ten days my mother was in the hospital.

Two days later, early in the morning, Jacky opened the door to insistent knocks to find a policeman we didn't know. He asked for John Graham Kilgour, Senior. Dad went to the door in his underwear.

"Mr. Kilgour, I'm sorry to have to bring you bad news. Your wife, Mary, passed away early this morning at McCook Hospital. Cause of death was pneumonia."

"Yes. We expected it. Thank you." The policeman left.

I was surprised to hear Dad say we expected it. It hadn't occurred to me that Mom would actually die. I thought she would recover eventually and return home, maybe after I was at Long Lane. No one close to me had ever died. But I had wished that she was dead, more than once, and now it had happened.

"You knew she was going to die, Dad?" I looked at him through eyes filling with tears. "Why didn't you tell us?" I hadn't meant it, not for her to really die.

"She was in a coma. The doctor said there was a chance she wouldn't come out of it."

I swiped at my eyes. "I didn't know what a coma was!" Could a wish come true?

Jacky said almost the same words as the nurse. "She was very, very sick. We knew that." He came close to me and whispered, "Don't make it worse. Let him be."

Dad got stone drunk fast and began crying. He wept without saying a word. The only sound came when he sniffled or blew his nose. It was the day before their twenty-fifth wedding anniversary. I cried too, alone in the car or in my half couch, from the sadness of it all. I never saw Jacky cry. But maybe he did.

*   *   *

Reverend Stevens helped arrange the funeral. I watched all of it intently. My mother's coffin was at the front of the long narrow room, surrounded by wreaths of white flowers. She had on the same navy blue dress she had worn to court and navy blue earrings I had never seen before. Her hair was arranged neatly, not a strand hanging loose as it did in real life. Make-up and lipstick and cheeks rosy with rouge made her look better than she had in years.

Dad wore a dark suit. Jacky wore a white shirt, blue tie and brown corduroy pants. I wore a navy skirt and matching sweater I had stolen and not returned. We sat on chairs alongside the coffin facing the rows of chairs for visitors. Some of the visitors, mostly neighbors, sat for a while looking sad or came to peer into the coffin and say to us, the family, that they were sorry. I thought, Sorry for what, sorry for what? Some of them came directly to us, not stopping to look at my mother. They must be afraid. I was too, but didn't want to show it. Not the guilt either, about wishing she was dead.

Mrs. Jones came, with Mr. Jones and Nancy. She had to take Mr. Jones's arm to make her way down the aisle. They knelt at the coffin and moved their lips, like Catholics do. Mrs. Jones held rosary beads. As they walked toward us, Dad stood up. Mr. Jones shook his and Jacky's hand. All the while Mrs. Jones held on to his sleeve. She came along and gave each a small awkward hug. She probably couldn't see us at all. When she reached me, she dropped her husband's sleeve and held me with both arms. It wasn't awkward any more. I could see tears in her eyes, which caused my own tears to overflow and run down my cheeks. I wished I could stay in Mrs. Jones's arms.

"Come talk with me when you can," she whispered before her husband took her arm and led her away. Nancy followed her parents with a scared look on her pretty freckled face, as if anticipating what it would be like to be in our shoes. It occurred to me that it might not be easy to have a blind mother, even one as nice as Mrs. Jones.

After the service we drove in the funeral director's car to Northwood Cemetery for the burial. A few of my mother's relatives from distant parts of New England came along to the cemetery. They were all elderly and not close to us anymore and they had their own family or health problems. They gave Jacky and me money, more than forty dollars each, and walked back to their car and left. It was a cold late November day with no breeze to shake free the few remaining dead leaves hanging from the trees. But the sky was a wonderful, brilliant blue.

I stayed out of school as long as I could. The neighbors brought us food. Mrs. Smart was nice to me. Mrs. Jones invited me into her apartment for a cup of hot chocolate and spoke fondly of the early years in the neighborhood when all the kids were little babies and toddlers and the mothers walked them in the park or sat on the front lawn gossiping. Mrs. Jones wasn't blind then. As she talked, she didn't cry as she had at the funeral.

"Was I born already?" I asked.

"At first it was my Nancy, Jacky, and a couple of other babies. You came along a few years later. The front yards had grass back then, not the dirt they have now." She had a pleasant look on her face remembering her own young motherhood, when she was healthy and active. "I remember holding you when you came home from the hospital. And walking with you while you learned to walk. Your hair was blonde and stuck out in all directions."

"It still does."

She laughed. "You had the prettiest blue eyes and chubby little cheeks. Your mother loved you a lot, you know."

Maybe in those early years, I thought.

"Your mother was a good woman, May. She really was, but she had too many burdens."

I didn't answer.

"Did you know your mother lost a baby girl? That was before Jacky."

"I think I heard something."

"She was stillborn. Born dead. It broke your mother's heart. You shouldn't judge her too harshly." Mrs. Jones looked at me with unseeing eyes. I didn't know what to say. My mother had a broken heart? Was that her problem?

After the funeral Dad stayed permanently drunk. Thanksgiving passed without celebration. In early December, he cashed the welfare check and bought his prescriptions and gallons of cheap port wine. In the absence of his wife, he gave me the remaining money to buy food for the rest of the month. I bought enough canned goods to last us the month and saved the rest to buy perishables as we needed them, because the refrigerator had stopped working some time ago. We had to have ice delivered once a week, the only ones on the entire street still using ice. That was something else that made us different. I tried not to be outside with the other kids when the iceman came.

I put my forty dollars from the funeral inside a pair of socks in my drawer to keep for an emergency.

CHAPTER 20

Dad

Back at school, when kids and teachers tried to talk to me about my mother, I changed the subject. What could I say? I missed her in a crazy kind of way, as if I missed what I never had, at least not for a long time. I didn't cry anymore.

The Juvenile Court hearing was supposed to be just after the funeral but Mrs. Smart had gotten it postponed until December 10. I had one week of freedom left.

I spent most evenings in the library, sitting in the large high school section now, able to read whatever I wanted. A few weeks after my mother's death, Mrs. Floyd sat down at my table and asked me how I was getting along.

"Everything's okay."

"If you need any help, will you let me know?"

My face froze into a blank pleasantness that was becoming a habit. "Sure." What could Mrs. Floyd do? What could anyone do? Mrs. Floyd probably didn't even know about the shoplifting and wouldn't be so willing to offer help if she did know.

That evening when I came home, Dad was asleep in the bedroom with the door closed, rather than in his kitchen chair. He had started using the bed more now that he was alone. Jacky wasn't there. For supper I heated up a tin of Vienna sausages and some baked beans and ate in the living room listening to music from the old radio. I fell asleep before Jacky came home, but woke enough to hear him when he came in.

The next morning he woke me up, poking me insistently on the shoulder.

"What're you doing, Jacky? Leave me alone."

"May, wake up." His voice sounded different, urgent.

"Huh? What?"

"Wake up. Daddy's dead!"

I sat up and rubbed my eyes. "What?"

"He must've had a heart attack. You'd better get up."

"Daddy's dead?" I started to cry.

"There's no point in crying. That won't help." He already had his Levis and a sweater on. Still barefoot, he sat on his cushions to pull on his socks and engineer boots.

"What're we going to do?"

"I don't know, but we're not going to be able to stay here. C'mon, get dressed."

I got up and put on jeans and a blouse. "Why can't we?"

"We're too young. I'm going to call the minister. You've got to start packing."

"Where is he?"

"The minister?"

"Dad!"

"In the bedroom. He's sitting on the edge of the bed."

"How do you know he's dead? Maybe he's sleeping."

"I touched him. He's cold."

I shivered. He had guts, my brother.

"Go in and get your stuff. We have to get ready."

"I'm not going in there alone. Come with me."

"He's not going to hurt you. He's dead!"

"Come with me anyway." He walked with me into the bedroom. Our father was slumped sideways from a sitting position on the edge of the rumpled bed in total stillness, gray whisker stubble covering his hollowed cheeks. His glasses perched crookedly on his forehead over sunken closed eyes. My stomach lurched and sent goose bumps shooting through my spine into my arms and head. This was my father, my Daddy. He must have died when he went to bed last night. Maybe he was already dead when I came home. I turned away, glad it was my big brother, and not I, who had found him.

I started pulling clothes quickly from hangers in the closet. I thought suddenly, nothing would be the same. Nothing. We had no parents. I grabbed all the clothes in my drawer in the bureau and went quickly from the dark, musty room. Jacky came behind me carrying two empty suitcases and shut the door, leaving our father alone.

"I'm going to call the minister. He'll know what to do."

"I'll go with you."

When we got to the gas station he gave me change to buy sodas while he made the phone call. I went into the shabby old station office that smelled of oil and men's sweat and poked hurriedly in the drink cooler's icy water to find two grape sodas. The owner, Hy, was in the garage and paid no attention to me, so I left the coins on the counter, opened the bottles, and ran out to Jacky at the phone booth.

"Okay, we'll wait for you. Yes. Thank you. Yes. Bye." He hung up and took a long swallow of soda.

"What did he say?"

"We should pack and wait for him at the apartment. He's going to call the funeral home. We're both staying with him tonight."

"Where does he live?"

"Off Ridgefield, near the park. I don't know how long we'll be there."

We swigged down the sodas, returned the bottles, and walked back to the apartment slowly, breathing in the cold morning air. I felt numb and sad, but my eyes were dry. It was after seven and turning light.

* * *

Over the next several days I felt small again. Others were in charge and I had no control over my own life. For one night Jacky and I both stayed with the minister, John, and his family, his wife Judy and their three kids, Rachel, Danny, and Linda. After the first night, Jacky went to stay with Ron. He came back once the minister and his wife sorted out where everyone would sleep. They moved their three kids into one large bedroom so I could have a room of my own. Jacky took the glassed-in heated porch where I had been sleeping.

My room had wallpaper with small roses on it against a white background and the wood trim was painted white. The bare wood floor was bright and clean, not dull and dirty like at the apartment. The room had its own closet and a double window looking out over the front porch. On a slant I could see the trees in the park, all barren for winter. If I wanted to run away I could easily climb out on the porch roof and slide down one of the round columns.

The minister told Jacky and me to go back to the apartment and take whatever we wanted. After that, everything would be sold and the money would be used to pay for the funeral. We got a good price from the funeral home in light of the circumstances, John said.

I wandered around the apartment feeling a little sorry for myself, looking at what I might take. There wasn't much. I pulled from the closet shelf a photo album with old brown and white portraits of us and black and white snapshots of us as children at the beach, with our older cousins, earlier pictures of our parents with distant aunts, and uncles. I found my mother's bead necklace, the one she had worn to court, and put it around my neck. That was the lone piece of jewelry in the small top drawer of the dressing table. I fingered her vanity set. Jacky came into the bedroom. He had the black metal box that held important papers under his arm. I pointed to the vanity set.

"Maybe I should take this."

"What good is that?"

"I don't know." The tortoise-shell comb teeth didn't bend or make a ping when I scraped them against my fingernail.

"It all looks pretty useless. Ugly even."

"You think so?" I ran the soft brush through the ends of my ponytail and put it back on the table.

Jacky sat on the bed already stripped of sheets. Had we done that? I couldn't remember.

"I'm not taking anything."

"Why not?"

"I want to forget this place. Forget them. I want to get on with my life."

"How can you forget your whole life, Jacky?"

"Well, I won't really, but why take reminders?"

"You're going to forget me too?"

"No, you and me are the good parts of this family. Don't worry. I won't forget you, even when I'm in the Navy."

"You promise?"

"Promise. Let's go. Take the album and let's get out of here."

I held the beads between my fingers, rubbing them like an Arab, or maybe a Catholic with a rosary. Maybe I should start fresh, too. I took them off and put them back in the drawer. I couldn't wear them in Long Lane, anyway.

I took one last glance at the bed our parents had slept in, at the chiffonier where they kept some clothes and Daddy's oval lawn bowling balls. Jacky and I used to leap from the top of it onto the bed when we were small.

My glance took in the bureau, the dressing table whose mirror had a BB hole made by Jacky aiming at me as I sat on the little shelf in front of the mirror. It had gone by my head at eye level about two inches to one side. Jacky had been so surprised when a BB flew out of the old gun that he had flung it to the floor and run crying into the kitchen to be comforted by Mom. I had been only two or three years old and didn't understand what could have happened, until our father came home from work and spanked Jacky hard with the wooden spoon while he yelled harsh words at him. I started to cry myself, knowing he hadn't meant to do it.

And there was the sewing machine piled high with junk now. One time Jacky ran the needle right through one of his fingers trying to fix it for our mother. It shriveled my stomach now to remember it. He had to go to Dr. Felder to have it taken out and the doctor had asked why he had brought along the thread and bobbin too. Mom hadn't thought to cut the thread. That was the same doctor who had refused to come to the house when Mom had pneumonia because we never paid him anymore.

Jacky left the key under the mat as usual, and then had to go back for it when he remembered we'd never return and the people dismantling the apartment wouldn't know where to look. He'd have to give the key to John to give to the undertaker.

I sat on the stairs inside the entry way waiting for him, remembering the times the neighborhood kids had played school and movies on those stairs on rainy days, the time the man came in and offered me and Joy Person a nickel to touch his pickle. We asked him for the nickel first, then ran screaming through the first floor hallway and out into the backyard. We bought five penny pretzels with his nickel and split them fairly. That had been stupid, but funny, too. Joy and I had been gutsier than I'd be now, after the Hog River.

* * *

At the funeral everyone was somber. The room, different from our mother's room, was crowded considering Dad had been sick so long that he had lost touch with his old friends. I didn't know some of the people. Maybe they were his doctors. Flowers scented the air, mostly white with touches of pale reddish brown and yellow with lots of frilly greens. Dad looked good in his black suit, his face shaved and his hair combed the way he used to let me do it. His face was peaceful, but white and waxy. It looked fatter than it had in real life. He had lost a lot of weight in the three weeks since Mom had died, but now you couldn't tell.

Neighbors hovered over us. Practically everyone in the two apartment buildings came, even old Mr. Edwards from the third floor. Of course, the Joneses came and I felt guilty about dragging Mrs. Jones out for these unhappy events. She hardly ever went beyond her back porch. Our teachers came, which surprised me. What a tragedy, I could hear people saying in low voices. How sad, two youngsters, so quick, both parents gone. Orphans, they whispered. I was an orphan. Should I feel different?

It got to be too much. I wasn't any different than the week before. Jacky and I had on the same clothes we had worn for our mother's funeral. My hair was in its same ponytail. Jacky and I sat near the coffin, surrounded with flowers and gloom. I found myself wanting to laugh. More than once I caught the same look on Jacky's face. He smiled at me, caught himself and pressed his lips into a flat line, and I did too. What would people think, especially the minister and his wife, who sat next to us and were respectable normal people?

Later in the afternoon, at Northwood Cemetery, our parents were buried about a hundred feet from each other, the closest they could be placed, the undertaker said. We went back to the parsonage to something like a party, with lots of food and people milling about. The entire first floor was filled with church people, neighbors, even our half-brother who showed up unexpectedly and shocked us by looking like a younger version of our father, complete with bright blue eyes, big nose, and gray bald head. We had never met him before. Already an adult with a wife and a small son, he seemed nice enough, but he didn't stay long. I wondered whether I should feel sorry for him for having been adopted and not being able to live with his father. After he left, Jacky and I went over to the park to get some privacy. We strolled along the red clay road at the top of Lookout Mountain until Jacky shouted, "C'mon, I'll race you!"

He started running and I took off after him. We laughed out loud as we ran, releasing what was inside us into the fresh air. At the bottom, lying on the cold dry grass, breathing hard, I had a sensation of release, of freedom, and I thought Jacky did too. But I took from my pocket the copies of the obituaries from the newspaper, sent to us encased in plastic, and read them while Jacky looked toward the sky. On one side was information about their lives and deaths.

Mary Cameron Fraser Kilgour, wife of John Graham Kilgour, Sr., died at McCook Hospital on November 18 after a brief illness. She was 50. Mrs. Kilgour was born in Dumbarton, Scotland. She went to Montreal, Canada, with her family as a young woman and came to the United States in the late 1920s. She was employed as a telephone operator before her marriage and then was a homemaker.

In addition to her husband, she leaves to mourn her a son, John, and a daughter, Mary, both of Hartford, and five sisters and brothers in Canada and the United States.

Dad's wasn't much different:

John Graham Kilgour, Sr., died December 8 of a heart attack after a long illness. He was 57. Mr. Kilgour was born in Dumbarton, Scotland, and came to the United States in the 1920s. He was self-employed and later worked for the Connecticut Trust Bank and the Porter and Company Stockbrokers before illness required him to retire.

His wife of twenty-five years, Mary Fraser Kilgour, predeceased him. A son, John, and a daughter, Mary, both of Hartford, and other relatives in Scotland and the United States survive him.

There was no mention of his first son. Maybe whoever wrote this didn't know about the boy originally named Graham John. On the other side was a cross and a prayer, the same for both of them.

Dear Lord, watch over your servant
And with loving kindness make easy
The entry into everlasting life.

Whether either of them would make it into heaven was a big question.

PART 2

Forks and Detours

CHAPTER 21

Glimpse of Light

I felt uneasy at the minister's house, which was always bustling with activity and goodness. Judy was a dietician and worked part-time in a hospital. The three kids, ages six, four, and two, were well behaved but too young to be much companionship. A woman named Norma from their previous parish helped out with the kids and the household chores and had a room in the attic. She was older than the Stevenses, maybe thirty or thirty-five.

John and Judy seemed alike to me, chubby and smiley. John's hair was darker and his eyes were a penetrating blue to Judy's amber brown. She had dimples that flashed when she smiled. They were both around my height, shorter than Jacky, who at seventeen had passed six feet already.

They tried to fit us into their family. Jacky agreed to give up his pin setting but he still worked at the supermarket. Between school and work he wasn't at home with them much. I had only school and was under orders to be home within an hour of the end of classes. The walk itself took almost half an hour, so I had little time to hang around the drugstore or library.

I was on a tight leash, in strange territory, still waiting to go to court, waiting for the future to come. There were chores to help with, but nothing unfair. The food was good and plentiful. Sitting at a formal table, saying grace, and following the table manners of John and Judy were unfamiliar and made me uncomfortable.

I mostly missed my freedom, not being able to come and go as I was used to. They insisted on knowing where I went and with whom. My major social activity became going to church: Sunday mornings and evenings and Wednesday evenings too. People at church were nice, but none of my friends or old neighbors went there.

I did get permission to go to the basketball games at the high school. I'd walk to the game and later go with friends to Gourson's for a soda or to the Jewish delicatessen for a piece of cheesecake with whomever was heading in that direction. John had to drive down to pick me up; he said it was too late to walk alone at night by the park. None of my new friends lived in that neighborhood. It didn't matter that I had walked alone all over town before; he said I couldn't any longer.

I couldn't smoke in the house or in John or Judy's presence. They said I was too young. Neither of them smoked.

Christmas passed, filled with religion and gifts nicer than I'd received in a long time. Strangers from church gave me things—talcum powder, books, puzzles, a hairbrush set, a neckerchief, a gold-colored cross and chain—gifts to the orphan, and part of me withered from their generosity.

I passed all my school subjects for the first semester, although just barely in two classes. Life fell into a pattern. But in ways I couldn't fully explain, it was unsatisfying. I became morose and quiet. Jacky saw it and tried to talk it out with me. It was February and still cold outside. We sat in his porch room, bright even on gloomy days, and talked.

"It's easier for you, Jacky. You'll be gone in four months."

"You can learn to like it here. They're trying their best to help."

"I know, but it's too much. It's too different. I need more freedom, to be by myself more."

"Well, you're not going to be able to have your old life here, that's for sure. These are normal people and they want you to behave like a normal girl."

"But I'm not a normal girl."

"But you could be if you wanted to."

No solution came out of these talks. If anything, they made me dig my heels in. Without really planning to, I started to rebel in small ways. I came in later from school. I wouldn't be at the entrance to the drugstore or the deli when John showed up after the basketball games, keeping him waiting while I smoked a last cigarette in the alley. On Wednesday nights I'd skip out of the church activities and go across the avenue to Gourson's or down to Maxwell's or the Dairy Queen. One day in early March, the first mild day after the long dreary winter, I played hooky from school and got caught. That evening John asked me what was wrong. He made a big deal out of it, as if playing hooky was a terrible thing. His face drooped in disappointment.

"Nothing."

"Are you sure? Can't I help?"

"No."

"Can Judy help?"

"No."

March fifteenth was my court date. The four of us drove together in John's station wagon. For the first time I turned right instead of left and entered the wood-paneled side of Juvenile Hall. In Judge Anderson's office, I sat alone in a chair directly in front of his massive desk. Jacky, John, and Judy sat behind a wooden railing in a row of chairs. Mrs. Smart sat by herself at a table behind me.

The room was quiet as the judge read through my file. He looked up from the papers and smiled, looking like a beardless Santa Claus. He looked over to the Stevenses and Jacky and smiled at them. He looked back at me.

"My job is easy today. Goodness, you've been through a lot in a short time. I think you've learned not to shoplift again. Correct?"

I slouched in my chair until the tip of my penny loafer touched his desk. I began rubbing the cleat against the wood, scratching it. He waited for an answer. I was wearing the gray pleated skirt and white blouse that only I knew were stolen.

"Yes."

"Reverend and Mrs. Stevens have agreed to take you into their home. You're being given an opportunity here. Do you think you can take it?"

I scratched again. The room became extremely quiet, so I stopped scratching. I imagined eyes boring into the back of my head, from Jacky, John, Judy, Mrs. Smart, all of them waiting for me to respond. Leave me alone, leave me alone, leave me…alone, I wanted to shout at all of them.

I shrugged. "I guess so."

"Sit up, young lady." Santa Claus became serious. "I expect you to comport yourself properly in my courtroom." Comport: another word like coma. I sat up and my toe could no longer reach his desk.

The judge released me into Reverend and Mrs. Stevens' custody. After the court hearing we went downtown to lunch. Jacky and I chose Honiss's. It had been my mother's favorite restaurant before things got bad. We used to go there after shopping trips downtown. We both ordered scallops, our parents' favorite. How odd, I thought, but Jacky and I didn't exchange even a secret glance.

"This is to celebrate May's rescue from Long Lane," John said and we chuckled even though it wasn't funny. I had forgotten the threat that had hung over me for so long. Now I wondered what it would have been like, compared to my life with the Stevens family. What kind of a lane was I on now?

I promised myself to behave better. Jacky asked me to. John included me in dinner table conversation. He wanted to know about my schoolwork , what I had done that day, the previous day. They did the same with their kids, Norma, and Jacky, if he was there. Judy tried to make conversation with me while doing housework or grocery shopping together. We all watched television together. This was the first time I had daily access to TV, but Judy picked the programs. The kids took baths every night and went to bed at eight. I had to take a shower every night and be in my room with light out by ten. These were new ways of living. Sometimes Judy had to remind me about the shower and to change my clothes each day.

I became acutely aware of how poor my earlier life had been. This made me angry, resentful, I wasn't exactly sure why, and I missed parts of that earlier life. I longed for the solitude of my father's dead car.

One day after three months and four days, a misunderstanding arose over a chore assigned to me that I neglected to do. Instead, I sat in my room reading while Judy worked alone in the kitchen. Norma had gone home to Pennsylvania for a vacation. Instead of obeying Judy's request to come help her, I stayed in my room. She got angry and told me so. Rather than get into an argument, even though I knew I was wrong and Judy was right, I left the house and went over to the park, where I walked alone for more than an hour, smoking one cigarette after another until I got too cold to stay out longer. I returned to the parsonage and went to my room without speaking to anyone. Soon John knocked on the door and asked me to explain myself. I didn't answer and eventually he went away. A while later, he came back and opened the door when I didn't respond to his knock.

"What's going on, May? Why did you refuse to help Judy?"

I didn't answer.

"We all have to help out, to play a role in the household, to make a family."

I stayed silent, staring a hole into the bedspread I was slouched on.

"May, you seem so unhappy. What is it? Do you want to leave?"

"Yes," I answered before I realized what I was saying.

"Are you sure?" He came in and sat at the end of the bed.

"Yes, I'm sure. It's not working out." I felt like I was floating free, saying the right thing somehow.

John sat for a while silently. Maybe he was trying to think of a solution. The room became so quiet I could hear him breathing and feel the tension. I crossed my arms and hugged them to my body and didn't say another word. He got up, walked to the door, and stretched himself to his full height as if trying to wake himself up. As he stood in the hallway he reached into his pocket for his handkerchief, took off his glasses and cleaned each lens slowly. He held them to the light in the hallway for inspection. He turned back toward me.

"You're really sure about this? Without knowing where you might go?"

"Yes, I'm sure."

I wasn't sure. I was running away from the present as I'd always done, but at least it was familiar. I heard John first on the phone in his bedroom next door and then thudding down the uncarpeted stairs. After a while his car crunched out of the driveway. I stayed in my room while the rest of the household went about its normal late Saturday afternoon life. I could hear cartoons playing on the TV in the living room. Chilly March air pushed through the inch of open window and I got up to close it.

Judy came to my room a little later, shortly after the phone had rung. She had been polishing silverware, the chore I was supposed to help her with, smelled metallic, and looked tired and flustered. She put a plate of chocolate chip cookies and a glass of milk on the bureau.

"In case you're getting hungry." Her voice was all one tone. "You need to pack your suitcase. John will be back soon to take you to Juvenile Hall." She closed the door with a soft click that echoed into my brain. It's final, I thought. It's happening. Something's happening.

I began to pack, numb and energized at the same time, glad I'd be gone before Jacky returned to try to talk me out of it.

On the ride to Washington Street, John asked me in several different ways why I was unhappy. Were they doing or saying the wrong things? Had the kids bothered me?

"It's not you."

"Then what is it?"

"I don't know. I wanted out."

"Out of what?"

"Your family."

"Why?"

"Any family, not just yours."

"I'm not sure I understand." He was silent as he drove through the traffic. He continued, "But that's okay. Will you call us if we can help?"

"Yes." I didn't understand it either. I just said what came into my head, but it was honest and somehow I knew it was what I had to say.

"Of course, Jacky will stay in touch."

He'd better. I couldn't imagine him not being there. Even though he wouldn't be there when he left for the Navy.

John parked the station wagon in the lot behind the building. "Let's pray before we go in." He took my hand and I let him. He was a good man, I knew that.

"Dear Lord, help this child to find the path she needs for a good and useful life. Watch over her as she makes her way. Give her Your protection and Your love. Teach her to love You and herself. In Jesus' name we pray. Amen."

CHAPTER 22

Detention

An elderly man let us in the back entrance, which led directly into a large old-fashioned kitchen. I stood there while John sat down at the table to sign some papers. There was a woman already at the table. She stood up.

"My name is Mrs. Dooley; this is Mr. Dooley. Come with me," the woman said to me. We walked into a large adjoining room where several kids watched a television on a shelf high on the wall. Otherwise it looked like a dining room with a linoleum floor and mismatched tables and chairs. The kids ignored us. I climbed a stairway behind Mrs. Dooley and went into a short corridor. To one side was a locked door she opened with a key.

"Go in."

I found myself in a smaller corridor. Mrs. Dooley went ahead and opened another door with a key and motioned me to follow her into a long narrow room with eight cots arranged in a row, four on each side of the door.

She pointed to the first bed to the left. "That one's empty. You can put your clothes in the locker next to it. The bathroom is there." She pointed to the other end of the room, to a closed door with "Bathroom" stenciled in white paint on the pebbled glass.

The room had high windows, above my head, each with a heavy mesh screen and a half-raised shade that let in the dim light of a streetlamp. It faced Washington Street at the front of the building. Glass globes hanging from the ceiling gave off a harsh light.

"Go ahead, empty your suitcase. I need to put it in storage." She stood watching me without expression as I put my things into the locker. I hadn't brought much, just clothes and shoes and the two obituaries. I had left my library books at the parsonage and hoped someone would think to return them.

"Now empty all your pockets."

I had jeans on and I reached into both front pockets and pulled out coins, a folded five-dollar bill, a pack of gum, my lucky azure-colored marble that looked like the globe, and a small comb. Mrs. Dooley herself took the pack of cigarettes from my blouse pocket and put everything in the suitcase and latched the lid shut.

"Put your hands on the wall and spread your legs."

I did as I was told, like a criminal in the movies. The woman ran her hands quickly over my body and I closed my eyes to the embarrassment of it. Then she took my arm and directed me out of the room before her. Her touch was not rough, but it told me who was in charge in case I hadn't figured that out.

Mrs. Dooley's gray hair was in a bun captured in a hairnet, like we had to wear in junior high cooking class. She also wore an apron over a housedress and white nurse's shoes with stockings rolled down around her ankles. My mother used to wear her stockings the same way. Mrs. Dooley unlocked a closet in the corridor and put the suitcase on a shelf. "I'm responsible for the girls this shift and my husband is in charge of the boys. We'll go back downstairs until bedtime. I'll introduce you to the others."

I walked in front of her, waiting while she unlocked and locked the doors. To the right of the stairs was another corridor.

"That's the boys' wing. It has two dormitories the size of the girls' dorm. And the schoolroom's up there." She pointed to another flight of stairs.

Downstairs, we went into the TV dining room and Mrs. Dooley announced my name to the five girls and three times as many boys sitting there, locked up like me. A few of them glanced my way and said hi with their hands before turning back to the movie, cowboys and Indians. I sat and watched for a while but it didn't hold my attention. My eyes strayed out the windows to the back of the building, but the scene was barely visible through the mesh. One of my ears could hear conversation from the kitchen but couldn't catch the words. I had the sensation of being alone but not uncomfortable in this crowd of kids. Whatever was going to happen would happen. I didn't have to change myself to make it happen.

My stomach rumbled. As I was thinking I'd have no supper that night, Mrs. Dooley came in with a plate of meatloaf, mashed potatoes, peas, a glass of milk, and a dish of canned sliced peaches. "You missed supper at five o'clock. I warmed this up for you."

* * *

The routine at the detention home was set in stone. We ate at the same times, morning, noon, and night. Except for school and recreation periods in the TV room, and meals in the same room, boys and girls were separated. We had different chores. The girls worked in the kitchen, helping with food preparation, cooking and setting the tables, and all the cleaning afterward. The boys cleaned the common rooms, corridors, offices, and their dormitory area. The girls cleaned our own dorm and bathroom. The boys also cleaned outside. I watched them smoking while they raked and swept.

New kids came almost every day and old ones left. No one stayed more than a few weeks. We weren't supposed to talk to each other about why we were there or where we thought we were going next. In fact, we weren't supposed to talk to each other at all. At night in the dormitory it was supposed to be silent time. And during meals the staff listened in and cut short some of the conversations by barking, "Inappropriate topic!" We were supposed to talk about such topics as sports and movie stars or books, and the immediate task we were doing, like "Give me the dish towel." Even then Mrs. Dooley would say, "Please. Say please." And we were supposed to respond, "Yes, Ma'am." This part of it, more than the locked doors, made me realize I was a prisoner. I couldn't speak when and how I wanted. But they couldn't stop me from thinking, so I spent my time daydreaming. And, of course, some of the girls did whisper to each other at night after lights out. None of their stories seemed terrible.

Every day the girls went for a walk in the neighborhood with the woman staff officer on duty. Usually it was Mrs. Dooley, sometimes Mrs. Stoner. By the end of the first week, I had talked Mrs. Dooley into letting us smoke on the walks, pointing out that the boys got to smoke outside while they did chores and it was too much to expect the girls to give up smoking cold turkey because we were in the juvenile hall. It had taken several days of convincing and when it worked I became a hero to the other girls, including two older sisters named Beulah and Hannah, in for fighting with a knife.

In this way, almost two weeks passed. Most of it was spring break from school, so there were no classes at the detention home. Finally, on a Friday morning, I was summoned to Mrs. Smart's office. She came right to the point. There was no studying of my file or writing.

"I'm disappointed it didn't work out at the reverend's, May. What happened?"

I shrugged, slouched in the chair, and remained silent.

"Well?"

I picked at a piece of lint on my skirt. "They were too nice." This came out of my mouth before I realized what I was saying.

Mrs. Smart smiled, showing teeth so straight they had to be false, like my father's. "Too much change in too short a time, perhaps?"

Maybe this was true.

"Girls your age have two choices. You're too old for the orphanage." I sucked in my breath. Even the thought of being in the same place those Hog River boys had been gave me the creeps. "You can go to Long Lane, which was the original plan. Or you can go to the House of Good Shepherd. Do you know about that place?"

"I know where it is, off Farmington, on Sisson Avenue." It was a few miles from my old neighborhood, big brick buildings set back from the street behind a tall wall of stone. We used to pass it on the way to Batterson Park and my father used to say I'd end up there if I didn't behave. It was a mysterious place from the street.

"The nuns run two homes for girls over there on Sisson Avenue. One, Marian Hall, is a locked facility for girls sent by their parents or by the court. The other, Euphrasia Hall, is the one we have in mind for you. It's like an orphanage for teenage girls. It's not a locked facility. You go out to school. You can continue going to Weaver if you want. Or you can transfer to Hartford High, which is closer."

Mrs. Smart took off her glasses and rubbed her eyes. "If you can't adjust there, you'll be sent to Long Lane. Is that clear?"

I nodded.

Mrs. Smart looked at me for a long time without speaking. I wanted to fidget but forced myself to sit still, to focus on what might be going through her mind, what she would say next. She could still change her mind and send me to Long Lane, or so I thought.

"Make sure that doesn't happen. Don't make a second mistake."

The same afternoon I was on my way to Euphrasia Hall, driven by a social worker I'd never met before. I was fourteen and a half and it was early spring, 1955, a time of peace and prosperity according to the magazines at Gourson's.

CHAPTER 23

The Hall

The social worker peppered me with questions as she drove through the traffic to Sisson Avenue. She could have gotten the answers from my file, which sat between us on the seat, already almost an inch thick. Her questions made it clear she hadn't read it. Good. The less she knew about me, the better. We drove along Farmington Avenue by Mark Twain's house, passing right by Woodland Street. I had a sinking feeling to know I had no reason to turn down that street. It was no longer my street.

I responded in clipped sentences to the social worker, polite but volunteering nothing, all the while thinking: What if I jump out of the car at a red light and run? Could I make it on my own? Summer is coming. Could I sleep in Keney Park?

I was startled out of these thoughts as the social worker braked to turn off Sisson Avenue into an entrance flanked on one side by the high stone wall I remembered and on the other by a chain link fence and row of pine trees. A small brass sign on the wall said Euphrasia Hall in fancy lettering.

I felt the tension build in me as I looked at the tall building directly in front of us, three stories of red brick, trimmed with gray stone. Its narrow side faced the tree-lined driveway from the street. On top of the entryway was an ornate gold cross. The social worker parked the car on a graveled section to the left and got out. I stayed where I was.

"Come on, we're here. You can't stay in the car."

She opened my door and bent down with a smile. What was there to smile about? My own face felt leaden, my body stuck to the seat, but I had no choice but to get out of the car and follow her.

We went up the concrete steps to a heavy green double door. Opening it, we found another set of stairs, these in marble or something like it. We climbed to another double door, this one ajar, and the social worker motioned me to the left into a reception room.

"Hello. I'm Mrs. Sloan from welfare. I've brought Mary Kilgour."

"Oh yes. We've been expecting you." The lady at the desk was white-haired and ancient, so pale her skin looked transparent. I could see her veins. But she smiled as her faded blue eyes sought us out, one after the other.

"I'm Miss O'Brien. Please take a seat."

Mrs. Sloan pointed me to a sofa and sat beside me. The old lady rose slowly and shuffled out of the room. It was painful to watch her.

I remembered entering kindergarten at the age of four, early due to the war, to free up mothers to work in the war industries. How afraid I had been, but my mother, who didn't work, held my hand and gave me courage. I wondered what Mrs. Sloan would do if I took her hand and held onto it.

We waited for several minutes, Mrs. Sloan finally opening up my file and leafing through the pages quickly. I longed to jump up and run out the door, down the double steps, along the shaded driveway to the street, anonymous, free. Could I blend into the neighborhood, find an empty garage, escape? End up in Wrong Lane?

There was a large picture of Christ on the wall with a staff and a flock of sheep. Was I to be one of the sheep? Another picture showed a nun with a book in her hand. She had a slight smile on her face like the Mona Lisa painting. What was the book? It was too small to be a bible. I could feel the pounding in my ears. Mrs. Sloan glanced my way. Could she hear it? She reached over and picked up my hand.

"You're nervous. Don't be. This is a pretty nice place. I think you'll like it here. But you'll have to give it time."

Before I thought to pull my hand away, Miss O'Brien returned with a nun dressed in long gowns of cream and white with a black hood covering her head except for her round, red face. She was dressed like the nun on the wall. A silver heart hung from a cord around her neck. God, she was scary looking. We stood up. The nun looked me in the eye through small rimless glasses. A lot shorter than I, she had to look up. But she was cool and calm and, like Mrs. Dooley, it was clear that she was in charge.

"I'm the superior of Euphrasia Hall. And that's Mother Mary Euphrasia, the founder of this religious order, in case you're wondering." She smiled and turned to Mrs. Sloan. "How are you, Lynn? Haven't seen you for a while."

"I'm fine, Sister, thank you. Here's Mary Kilgour. She goes by May. I'm hoping she'll do well here."

"I'm sure she will. Do you have her file?" Mrs. Sloan handed her the folder from the car seat. "Fine. I don't think we need to take more of your time. I know how busy you social workers always are."

"Yes, Sister, too many kids, too few workers. It's always the same. Write your congressman." She smiled and the nun chuckled. "Goodbye. Behave yourself, young lady. I don't want to have to come back for you and make that long drive to Long Lane." Her voice sounded stern but she winked and gave my arm a pat. I watched her walk out the door, down the steps to the second door and away, and was struck by a crazy sense of abandonment.

"Come with me, dear." My mind clicked back. I picked up my suitcase and followed the nun, my mouth dry with apprehension. As we went into a small office, everything telescoped to tiny size, as happened to me from time to time. I had to concentrate on where I walked and what the nun said. A flash of light wherever I looked obliterated the nun's face and the rug in front of her desk, and it bounced back like a fierce sun from the window behind the desk.

"Sit down, dear. You didn't bring much with you, I see. But I understand your brother will be bringing your other things tonight. He's coming for a visit." I could feel my face light up. The nun smiled. "He'll be here at seven thirty. Let me tell you a little about us."

As the nun talked, the flashing light disappeared and the room gradually returned to normal size. I was so happy to hear Jacky would be coming that I half-listened as she told me about Euphrasia Hall and the religious order that ran it.

"I understand you're a Protestant and have been living with the pastor of your church. No one here will try to convert you to Roman Catholicism, but we will expect you to follow the rules and to attend your own church on Sundays. Do you have any questions?" I shook my head. "Well then, let me show you around."

We walked to the third floor. My loafers with cleats on the heels and toes banged against each metal stair. The nun in rubber-soled black lace-ups walked silently.

"This is where the schoolgirls live." She pointed out a shower room as we passed, another room with toilet stalls and sinks, and an ironing room with a big wash tub and a row of ironing boards as we walked further along a wide corridor of gleaming wood. Closed wood doors stood out from the white walls at regular intervals. The ceiling was high. Light fixtures on the high ceiling provided a soft light.

"The working girls live on the second floor. All is quiet now, but it won't be once the girls are home from school or work. You'll have a roommate. After a while, if you earn it, you might be able to have a private room."

Toward the end of the corridor there was an open double door into another corridor.

"This used to be a dormitory but we partitioned it into double rooms since almost all our girls are teenagers. Here's your room."

We went into a pale blue room on the left. It had two single beds with white metal frames and other furniture. A closet had been built against the entry wall. At the other end of the room, sunlight streamed through a large window. I walked over and looked down on a pretty garden.

"That's the Magdalene sisters' garden. When they're using it, it would be courteous not to look out at them. They're a cloistered order of sisters who devote their lives to religious contemplation and helping us run this property." I must have looked perplexed because the nun continued. "Cloistered means they don't go out into the world. They stay in their convent and lead lives of prayer and physical labor."

I nodded, as if this made sense to me.

There were no bars or mesh on the window. In the distance, across the garden and lawns thick with trees was a fenced-in area and another large brick building. Through the tree branches I could see a swimming pool.

"That's Marian Hall. You needn't concern yourself with that, dear. Settle yourself in now. Your roommate is Frances Shea. She should be home within the hour and will introduce you to the other girls. If you have any questions, come downstairs and ask Miss O'Brien." At the doorway she stopped and smiled. "The girls call me Mother."

Yeah, sure, calling a nun Mother? Fat chance. I'd already had one mother and that was plenty. I watched the short, stout nun walk down the corridor. Then I went back into the room and closed the door. There was no lock. I couldn't lock anyone out, but they couldn't lock me in, either. I went to the window and looked again at the garden. The earth in the flowerbeds had already been turned for spring planting. I expected the window to be permanently locked, but it opened easily and I leaned my head out to sniff the garden air. It was a long way to the ground and the outside of the building was smooth brick—no footholds to use to climb down or up.

Two bureaus stood side by side. One had photographs, a brush and comb, and other odds and ends on top. The other was empty. I hung some skirts and blouses on empty hangers in the closet and put the rest of the things from my suitcase into the top drawer, tucking the two obituary cards into the pile of underwear. There were white sheets and towels, a tan blanket, and a dark blue cotton bedspread on the bed near the door. I made the bed the way Judy had taught me. Now the two beds matched. The chairs and desks were painted bright red. The empty one near the door must be mine. My own desk for my own things, something I'd never had.

The room was clean and neat. Maybe that was a rule. I lay on the bed and let my mind drift. It went from the detention home cot, to the flowered room in the parsonage, to my couch in the apartment. I tried to remember the wallpaper. Had it been country villages on a yellowed landscape? Little people? Becoming unhinged from that life, except for Jacky, I became drowsy thinking about seeing him that night. I must have fallen asleep because I was startled by someone bursting through the door.

"Oh, sorry, didn't know you were sleeping. Mother said you'd come." This must be my roommate. She was short and thin with curly blonde hair. "I'm Francie."

She leaned back out the doorway. "Hey everybody, new girl's here!" Within seconds, several girls around my age filled the room. They sat on the beds and chairs, on the floor, or leaned against the walls.

They all talked at once. I answered questions but mostly listened, part of the group and alone at the same time. Several of them had been at the detention home and asked about Mr. and Mrs. Dooley and the others. After a while they drifted away and I was alone with Francie.

"How old are you?"

"Fourteen."

"What grade are you in?"

"Ninth."

"You must be smart. I'm in eighth at Noah Webster and I'm fifteen. I stayed back a year when I was moving between foster homes. Where's your stuff?"

"My brother's coming tonight with it."

"How old is he?"

"Seventeen."

"Is he cute?"

I shrugged. "I guess so."

"Do you have a boyfriend?"

"No. You?" Gosh, this girl was more talkative than I was.

"Yeah. His name's Joe. I'll introduce you."

"How long have you been here?"

"Four months. Before that I was in six different foster homes, plus three weeks in the detention home. I haven't lived with my folks for almost three years."

"Where're they?"

"Here in Hartford, behind G. Fox."

She didn't say why she didn't live with them and I didn't ask. I didn't want to tell her too much about myself. I said my parents were dead and left it at that. So did she.

At five thirty a bell rang and we went to the dining room for supper. It was a brightly decorated room in the basement but the upper wall had windows on two sides at ground level. A couple of them were open to let in the fresh evening air. Small tables were scattered around the room and some lower round tables encased poles that went up to the ceiling. The round tables and the posts they surrounded were painted different colors, and had comfortable-looking padded lounge chairs gathered around them.

While we stood in the food line, Francie pointed out the chores list on the bulletin board.

"We all take turns, setting up, serving, and washing dishes, cleaning bathrooms, showers, the corridors, stuff like that. And each girl has to take care of her own room. It's not too bad."

"How many kids live here?"

"More than a hundred, I think, counting the working girls. They eat later."

We took two seats at an empty table and began eating. Two girls wearing parochial school uniforms, Barbara and Sandy, joined us and the talk turned to school and boys and the new music in the jukebox. I mostly listened and ate. The food was good: grapefruit juice, spaghetti and meatballs, salad, milk, Jell-O with a dab of whipped cream for dessert.

After supper we went to the library for study hall, six thirty to seven thirty. I had to go to the library even though I didn't have any homework. The nun in charge, a young one who said her name was Mother Edward, told me to choose a book to read and be quiet.

"Why does she have a man's name?"

"It's a saint's name. Be quiet or we'll have to stay extra," Francie whispered.

I selected a book about saints from one of the bookshelves lining the wall. The library ran the width of the building. Three sewing machines took up one corner. I hoped they didn't require sewing. I'd almost flunked it in eighth grade for cutting slits into my finished skirt fabric while taking out the basting stitches.

The other girls were studying or reading for real, although one or two caught my eye and smiled. I skimmed the book about saints looking for Edward and found two. One was a martyr priest who was hanged. The other, called the Confessor, was king of England. It seemed odd that a nun would identify with them. Weren't there any saintly females she could identify with? I looked up Saint Euphrasia. This was an odd one: a five-year-old girl who was promised in marriage to a senator but became a nun in Egypt instead. It didn't square with what the Mother Superior had said about the nun who started the Good Shepherd Sisters in France in the nineteenth century. Maybe the Good Shepherd Euphrasia wasn't a saint? She had taken the saint's name because she identified with a child who became a nun rather than get married? Did this have something to do with the unwed mothers my father said used to be sent to the House of Good Shepherd?

It occurred to me that I might be embarking on an adventure right here in Hartford.

CHAPTER 24

Jacky

At seven-thirty, the tinkling of a bell released us from study hall and I went down the stairs two at a time to Miss O'Brien's office. Jacky was in the same spot I'd sat in that afternoon. He looked awkward surrounded by three grocery bags and a suitcase, with Jesus and Mother Euphrasia hovering over him. When he saw me, a wave of relief crossed his face and he stood quickly to give me a hug and a kiss on the cheek. He was getting so tall I had to reach up to kiss him.

"John drove me over."

"Is he still here?" I didn't want to see John. I wanted Jacky to myself tonight. I hadn't seen him for more than two weeks. Only parents could visit at the Detention Home, and I hadn't been able to convince them Jacky should count since I didn't have any parents.

"No, he left. I'll take the bus back."

He was wearing the plaid flannel shirt I'd given him two Christmases ago. It was open over another shirt, the sleeves partly rolled up. It probably didn't fit him any more but it was nice of him to wear it, knowing I'd remember.

"What a nice shirt, Jacky!" I grasped his upper arm and felt him tighten his bicep muscle.

"It's my very favorite one of all the many I own." He laughed.

I put the bags and suitcase behind the reception desk. Miss O'Brien wasn't there. An older girl in her seat said it was okay. We went downstairs to the dining room, which was cleared of supper and being used as a recreation hall. I had already learned it was called the gym. The jukebox just inside the door played a Perry Como record and four girls played Ping-Pong at a table in one corner. I chose a table in the opposite corner where we could talk quietly. I could feel the other girls' eyes on us, especially on Jacky.

We talked almost as if we were continuing a conversation from the previous day, which was how it always was with us, so comfortable with each other the absences weren't real absences. Or something like that, anyway.

"How was the detention home?"

"Not too bad. I'm glad I'm out, though, and not in Long Lane."

"Yeah. This place seems better. The grounds are nice, at least what I could see in the dark. You like it okay?"

"So far it's okay. See that girl over there by the Ping-Pong table, the one with blonde hair? She's my roommate, Francie. She has parents but they live on Front Street."

"Is she nice?"

"Seems to be. What've you been doing?"

"Nothing much. School, work, church, getting ready to join the Navy. I'm doing push-ups and sit-ups and running in the park. Boot camp is pretty tough."

"Yeah, your arm muscle felt really hard. You want me to punch you in the stomach?"

He stood up. "Go ahead, as hard as you can. C'mon."

"I was joking! Sit down. You'll get me in trouble." I laughed. "How are Ron and your other friends?"

"Good. Everyone's fine."

"How about work?"

"The same. Remember Sam Greenwood?"

"I don't think so."

"Well, he got fired for stealing a whole bunch of stuff out the back door of the store right into a friend's car. They're pressing charges too."

"How old is he?"

"Already eighteen, although they say he won't do jail time. Just probation."

"Hmmm. He must have good parents."

Jacky chuckled. "Probably. But you got sprung, so don't worry about that anymore."

"Yeah. Have you seen any of my friends around?"

"Nope. I haven't seen any of them."

After a while we were quiet together, comfortable, listening to the music. He pulled out his cigarettes. "Do they allow smoking?"

I pointed to the ashtray. "I guess so."

He lit a cigarette and offered me one, which I practically grabbed. "You out?"

I nodded and told him about the limits on smoking at the detention home. One pack lasted me the whole two weeks.

"Take the pack. I can get some more at the drugstore."

We smoked in silence. I took a deep drag of the unfiltered brand he smoked. Too harsh for me, I preferred filtered Kents when I bought my own.

We have different homes from each other now, I thought. Will we grow apart? I had accepted the idea he would be physically gone when he went into the Navy, but already? The music interrupted my thoughts. Girls were dancing together and singing along with Bill Haley and the Comets, "Rock Around the Clock."

One of the girls came over to Jacky. "Want to dance?"

"No thanks. I haven't seen my sister for a while." He smiled and she smiled back before walking away giggling.

She had probably been dared to approach him. These kids must think Jacky's cute, I thought. I guessed he was and he had a way with girls. I remembered the girls from church, how they had flirted with him and he had flirted back. I gazed at him while he watched the dancers and was proud that he was my brother. He was almost eighteen, tall and slender with dark brown hair he wore in a crew cut. He never got pimples like I did. His eyes were light brown and his nose was straight, not too big not too small. It didn't have the bump mine had, which I got from our father. Jacky took his coloring and features more from our mother. Yet many people told us they could tell we were brother and sister. I liked to hear that. It was funny how we never fought with each other anymore, like we did when we were younger. I had usually been the instigator, prodding him to retaliate and get in trouble with our parents, who had warned him boys do not hit girls, he was my older brother and should protect me. That had been long ago, when our parents taught us things, but I thought Jacky had learned the lesson well.

"John and Judy said to say hello. The kids too. Judy put a tin of home-made fudge for you in one of the bags."

"That was nice. Tell her thanks." I remembered Judy's fudge. We had made it together at Christmas and it was much better than store-bought.

"They feel badly about what happened, you know."

"It wasn't their fault. Would you tell them that for me?"

He nodded. He looked over at the Ping-Pong table, empty for the moment.

"Do you want to play?"

We hit the ball back and forth but didn't keep score. After a while, Jacky looked at his watch. "It's after nine o'clock. I'd better go if I'm going to catch the bus."

"When're you coming again?"

"How about next Saturday night? The nun said you could go out to eat with me. We can visit each other every week. I'll come about seven o'clock, straight from work. Okay?"

"Okay, good. I'm starting back at Weaver on Monday, so I might see you in school before then."

I walked him out to the front stoop and hugged him good-bye. I watched him walk toward the street, in alternating shadow and light as he passed under the wrought-iron lamps edging the path. He strode straight and tall, no longer the hunched, skinny boy with ragged hair and circles under his eyes. Seeing him every week would be good. I was happy about that.

*   *   *

Life fell into a pattern of long bus rides to and from Weaver, hanging around with the other schoolgirls, meals, study hall, and weekly visits with Jacky. The day after I arrived, my name was on the monthly chores list to help wash and dry dishes for a week, set up and clear the tables for two weeks, and clean the shower room for a week. None of these chores, shared with other girls, took more than a half hour a day. I kept my half of the room clean and got along well with Francie. The other girls took a shower every day so I did the same. It wasn't a habit only of the Stevens family.

We played softball on the front lawn after school and played the juke-box and danced in the gym. I got pretty good at Ping-Pong but five or six of the girls could still beat me. We tried to stay out of the way of the nuns and broke the rules in small ways. We hung out in the apple orchard on the south side of the building, smoking and talking. We sauntered around the back road circling the property, passing close to the fenced yard of Marian Hall. If the girls were out, we threw cigarettes over to them and waved.

Occasionally arguments and even physical fights erupted between the girls, which led to restrictions, staying in their rooms, or not being allowed to go out on weekends. Jacky's visits were too important to me to jeopardize by fighting. He would be leaving for the Navy in three months. Besides, I had no reason to fight with anyone. Nobody made me mad. When I needed to be alone, I went to the library and read. It became for me the hideaway my father's old green Ford had been.

When Jacky came on Saturdays, we went to one of the small restaurants or the drugstore lunch counter on Farmington Avenue to eat and talk. We talked for hours and never ran out of topics. The conversations had a lazy, unrushed quality to them even when we became earnest, debating this or that in the newspaper or on TV. We talked about school and friends; current events; the Navy, which Jacky had learned a lot about; and books I was reading. From time to time our life at 416 Woodland came up, but mostly we stayed in the present and future. We asked each other questions and listened intently to the answers. Jacky shared his feelings about a new girlfriend, his first who didn't go to Weaver or the church. He seemed shy and proud about her at the same time.

"I do believe you're smitten, Jacky Graham!"

"Smitten? Jacky Graham? Where'd you get words like that? Out of one of your true love magazines?" He laughed and screwed up his face.

"Okay. Are you in love, then?"

"No, she's just a girl for this port. There'll be many others." His mind was on the Navy.

Jacky paid for our Saturday night outings and also got in the habit of giving me five dollars each week from his pay from the First National. "This is so you won't steal," he told me. And I didn't.

CHAPTER 25

Francie

Francie became my best friend. Although we went to different schools, we hung around together in the gym and outside on the grounds as the weather warmed up. We ate together most nights and sat at the same table in study hall. She reminded me in many ways of both Joanie and Stella but she had a livelier sense of humor than either of them. Sometimes the two of us would lie in bed at night telling each other stories that would send us into fits of laughter so loud and long that the patrolling nun would come into the room to tell us to cut it out. We had the same funny bone and Francie brought out a comic side in me that felt new and familiar at the same time, as if it had always been there, unused.

One Saturday afternoon when a bunch of girls went downtown to a movie, Francie invited me to go with her to visit her parents. The other girls took the bus home but we walked through the narrow downtown streets on the far side of Main Street toward the Connecticut River until we reached a rundown neighborhood known for its crime and poverty: Front Street. It was a notorious neighborhood, often discussed in the newspapers and much worse than my own old neighborhood. I had never known anyone who actually lived there. Years later it was all torn down for urban renewal.

At a brick building with a grocery store on the ground floor, we went into a narrow stairway and climbed to the third floor, to the Sheas' apartment. Both of her parents were home. They seemed surprised to see her, greeted her courteously, but more like she was a neighbor stopping by than a daughter, and her father quickly went into another room and closed the door. We sat and had a cup of coffee with Mrs. Shea. While Francie and her mother talked about Francie's older brothers and sisters, I looked around the room. It reminded me of 416 Woodland on its best days. It was cleaner and brighter. Who would have thought that a slum apartment on Front Street would be nicer than my family's apartment?

We left after only twenty minutes. As we walked back up to the Old State House to catch the bus, I wanted to ask Francie about her family, but decided to wait and let her raise it. Just before we reached the bus stop, with its crowd of waiting passengers, she did.

"I'm not supposed to have any contact with them. And that's all I want to say."

I nodded and kept quiet. It crossed my mind that I would like to give Francie a bag of pistachio nuts.

*   *   *

About three months after I arrived at The Hall, on a Friday evening, Francie had one of her usual dates with her boyfriend, Joe. This time, she told me a few days ahead of time that Joe had a friend he could fix me up with if I wanted.

"Sure, why not. Is he cute?"

"Not bad, and he's nice. His name's Roger. He goes to Hartford High. Marlene is going with us too, with a guy named Paul."

Francie spent a full hour getting ready. She took a shower, washed and dried her curly hair, and put more make-up on her face than I'd ever seen anyone do.

"Do you want to borrow any of this make-up, May?"

"Nah. I'll just use lipstick."

"Okay. Maybe when we're not going out I can show you how to do this. Our coloring's about the same."

Francie wore a tight black skirt and a pink blouse with the collar up and the top two buttons undone. Outside the wall she undid the third button. Marlene wore long slender black slacks accentuating her slimness, but a frilly white blouse softened the effect. She had on make-up too, although not as much as Francie. I, with my plaid skirt and blue sweater, felt like the chaperone, even though I was the youngest of the three.

I had to admit Francie looked good—at least seventeen or eighteen.

It was spring and the evening was pleasant. The tall trees lining the driveway were full with new growth and the grass was a bright young green. We walked over to Park Street, a neighborhood called Frog Hollow, and met up with the three boys, who all lived in that run-down neighborhood of apartments above stores on treeless streets. Only Roger went to school. The others had already dropped out and worked, or tried to. Roger seemed nice enough except he was majoring in shop and still getting Ds, and had big pores on his nose. We went to a pizza parlor to eat and hang out. The boys drank beer out of paper bags. Francie and Marlene were drinking too. That made me uncomfortable. I drank my usual Coke.

Fifteen minutes before the ten thirty curfew we all piled into Joe's blue Chevy for the ride back to The Hall. We were too squeezed together to pair off for necking but Roger managed a short wet kiss and tried to touch my breast. I pushed his hand away and kept my mouth closed. The car stopped on the street outside the wall.

Joe said, "I'll let you girls out here. That place is too spooky."

"Yeah. I went in there once," said Marlene's date, Paul. "The nun hated me even though I didn't do anything."

"She hated you because she smelled trouble, Paulie," Joe said. "But the nuns scare me too, I admit that."

By now I had learned many of the people in the neighborhood thought The Hall was as mysterious as my family had once thought. The ladies on the crosstown bus I took to school in the morning, all insurance company employees who had ridden the same bus for years, asked what it was like in the House of Good Shepherd. I often noticed cars slowing to look through the fence and row of pine trees, especially if the girls were out playing on the front lawn, as if we were freaks on display. Bad girls, maybe, like my father used to say.

No one, including myself, defended the nuns, though I at least had stopped thinking of them as spooky. Marlene and I climbed out of the car and walked up the driveway. Francie said she didn't want to go in yet. We left her, thinking she wanted to make out with Joe or sober up a bit. She was pretty groggy in the front seat, whispering with Joe and shaking her head no.

Mother Superior sat in the reception room checking the girls off the sign out/sign in sheet.

"Where's Francie?"

"She'll be here in a minute. Just wanted to say goodnight to Joe," I said. Marlene didn't say a word or look at Mother directly. She signed in quickly without breathing and left the room.

"I don't know what she sees in that fellow. He doesn't have a steady job, doesn't go to school. Well, it's past curfew. She's going to be restricted if she isn't walking into the building as we speak."

"Maybe she doesn't have her watch on. Do you want me to go out to the car and get her?"

"Yes, dear. Please do that."

I walked outside and down the driveway, wondering if I was becoming a goody two-shoes and if Francie would be annoyed with me. But the car was gone! I looked both ways and turned around to see if they had driven up the driveway after all. No sign anywhere of the blue Chevy or of Francie. I walked back into the building, wishing I could produce her from the TV room and be able to tell the nun that Francie had gotten in on the stroke of curfew and had simply forgotten to sign in.

Instead, I had to say, "She's not there. The car's gone."

"Are you sure?"

I nodded. "I looked up and down the street and on the side of the building."

"Okay, dear. Go to your room."

As I left the reception room I heard her say to Sister Edward, "I'll give her half an hour before calling the police."

Damn, I hated to see Francie get in trouble. She already had two weekend restrictions this month for mouthing off. Francie had more energy than she knew what to do with on top of that funny, mischievous streak I liked. I walked up the metal stairs to the schoolgirls' floor, read a novel about the French revolution called *Desiree* for a while, and fell asleep alone in our blue room.

The next day was Saturday. Francie's bed hadn't been slept in. I worried as I worked in the kitchen setting out the breakfast cereals, milk, and juice, and chopping vegetables for a lunch salad. On my midmorning break I looked for Marlene and found her in her room painting her toenails. She knew nothing.

In the early afternoon, Francie finally showed up with Joe. He parked on the street in the same spot as the previous night and walked onto the property with her. Watching from the open window in the TV room, I saw Joe pushing Francie ahead of him as if to encourage her to go into the building. She was drunk. I felt my stomach turn over. Mother Superior stood on the top step outside the door. They got to within ten feet of the steps.

The nun said, "Come in, Francie. You're already in serious trouble. Don't make it worse."

Francie hugged Joe and whispered. He shook his head. She giggled and nodded her head up and down fast. Her pretty skirt and blouse from the night before were all wrinkled and sad-looking.

"Fuck you, Mother," Francie shouted.

The words rang out shockingly clear in the still afternoon. I looked at the nun's face to see how angry she was. From the side her face didn't change at all. I considered that she didn't know what the word meant. No, that couldn't be possible. Francie turned and ran back along the driveway toward Joe's car, her blonde curls bouncing in the air, looking like a small child except for the wobble in her gait. Joe didn't seem to know what to do and looked at the nun with a plaintive shrug.

Mother Superior turned her back on him and came into the building. I could hear her telephoning from the reception room, asking that Frances Shea be picked up and taken to Long Lane; she was no longer welcome at Euphrasia Hall.

I sat alone in the TV room, thinking about what had happened. My roommate sent to Long Lane. It was easy to screw up here. Francie had liked The Hall, at least had put up with it. She said she preferred it to all her previous foster homes. Now what?

I went outside and walked to the street. No one stopped me. I could have kept going. I stood at the curb for several minutes watching for the blue Chevy, feeling anxious for Francie, annoyed with her, sorry for her for making the choice she had made. It was dumb!

Sure enough, word came back that the cops picked up Francie and took her to Long Lane, and she'd probably be there for three years, until she turned eighteen. Just for drinking beer and staying out overnight, on top of whatever she had done before coming to The Hall. It had happened so fast. One day she was a schoolgirl having fun, enjoying her freedom. The next day she was locked up in Wrong Lane, and who knew what would happen to her.

That could happen to me, I thought, as I lay in bed over the next couple of nights. I thought about how I'd liked Francie, about how I wished she were still here as my roommate to share things with, and about where I had come from and where I might end up. The boy I'd had the date with the night Francie messed up her life called for another date but I said no. I'd stay away from those Park Street boys.

PART 3

Upward

CHAPTER 26

Choices

School finished for the year. I turned my report card in to Miss O'Brien as required. A week later, after supper in the gym, Mother Superior called me over to the desk where she or one of the other nuns sat to monitor the room, although usually they paid more attention to their small book of prayers than to us.

"I've looked at your report card, dear. All Bs are better grades than you had when you came. But you can do much better."

Did I need this conversation? I was still smarting over the loss of Francie. "I guess it depends on the courses I have."

"No, it depends on you. You're blessed with a good mind and you're a hard worker."

I slid down on the tan, vinyl lounge chair at the unexpected praise. I crossed one knee over the other and swung my foot, nervously at first, but it soon picked up the rhythm of the jukebox song, "Mr. Sandman."

"Next year you should aim for all As. I'll bet you can do it just by using the library study hour to your best advantage." The nun looked over her rimless glasses at me. "And by taking yourself seriously, as a young lady with a future."

I felt my face grow hot. The jukebox went silent. My foot stopped swinging and I uncrossed my legs.

The nun opened the desk drawer and pulled out a small box. "Here, this is for you."

I opened the box to find a small silver medal on a silver chain. It had the likeness of the nun on the wall in the reception room, Sister Mary Euphrasia. I looked at it, at all the detail, just like in the painting, turning it between my fingers a few times, not knowing what to say. It was real silver. I put it around my neck.

"Thank you, Mother." There. I'd said it. It hadn't been that hard. It sounded all right. Not Mom, but Mother.

"You're welcome. Keep it up." She reached inside her complicated gowns and pulled out a quarter. "Here, play some Bing Crosby."

*   *   *

Jacky continued to come most weekends. He had a new girlfriend, more serious even than the last one. Her name was Marie.

Jacky and I had taken to talking about our parents. Not often, but occasionally. From comments he let slip, I came to realize that being the strong older brother for me hadn't been as easy as he'd tried to let me think. The longer he stayed at the Stevens' house, maybe the more he was able to act like a seventeen-year-old, the more he was able to admit that the past had sometimes been hard for him too.

We also talked about religion, not so much about specific practices of Methodists or Catholics, but about more basic things—whether God existed, and if not, what started it all. We started following current events. Both of us became more aware of violence overseas that might involve Jacky once he joined the Navy. There were problems in Guatemala and Iraq and Vietnam. We'd look up these places in one of the almanacs on the drugstore's magazine shelves. Sometimes he'd bring the almanac to our table, open it at a random page, and read some exotic new information. I asked him if he had finally gotten the reading bug but he denied it.

His graduation day came at the end of June, and the ceremony was held in the Bushnell Memorial Auditorium downtown. I gave him a silver identification bracelet engraved with his name, John Graham Kilgour, leaving off the junior he used to be. After the ceremony, he dropped me back at The Hall and went to a party with kids his own age. He left for the Navy early the next morning.

I had been working in The Hall's kitchen after school and on weekends and had used my pay to buy Jacky's gift. I helped the cook, Josefina, by peeling vegetables, stirring cooking pots, making Jell-O and cakes, and washing pots and pans. It paid enough for me to buy the things The Hall didn't provide and would replace Jacky's five dollars once he left for the Navy. I learned that social security survivors' benefits, not welfare, paid my basic room and board at The Hall, and I was pleased about not being on welfare, even though officially I was a state ward and the governor, of all people, was my guardian.

* * *

Each summer, the girls of The Hall used a private lake owned by rich friends of Mother's. Happy Lake was a magical place and I always asked for time off from the kitchen on the day we went. There was a small house with a kitchen, bathroom, and covered patio on the lake's shore. Woods surrounded the small lake and we seldom saw anyone else. The water was a placid blue-green, the sky a brilliant blue. We had use of a rowboat, a canoe, and a wooden raft anchored in the middle of the lake. Attached to the raft was a military-style rubber life raft with a webbed bottom. We could sit in it and be covered with water. I always brought a book with me but also came to know the other schoolgirls well by lazing about with them on the raft, paddling the canoe around the perimeter, and grilling hotdogs and hamburgers for lunch.

Each girl had a story. Few were real orphans like I was. Most had little or no contact with their parents and had been in many foster homes over the years, like Francie, moved by the state or the foster parents, or by their own misbehavior, sometimes intentional. The experiences had usually been bad. They told about beatings, neglect, and sexual abuse. Some foster homes were good and some foster parents better than others; but many did it for the money they earned for keeping foster children. Their stories made me realize that John and Judy Stevens had been extraordinarily good foster parents.

The worst of all things about foster care for most of the girls was the lack of permanence, and that was what they liked most about Euphrasia Hall. It was always there. The nuns might change, and the younger ones did, but the place itself, the building, other girls, and the routines were always there. They could stay there until they were grown. Unless they screwed up, of course, as Francie had. Yet the rules were clear and fairly easy to follow. Another thing about The Hall they liked, and I realized I liked it too, was the ability to be with others and yet hide within the group to get personal space. This wasn't always possible in a crowded family setting like an individual foster home.

Of course, it was the kids who had problems in foster care who ended up at The Hall. There were probably other kids out there who could adapt and be happy in foster families.

Some of the girls at The Hall had parents they still saw regularly but for one reason or another couldn't live with them. Some had brothers and sisters scattered in different homes, although there were two pairs of sisters at The Hall and the nuns encouraged family visits when it was possible. One girl had been abandoned on the steps of a church as a newborn. She had lived in foster homes all her life but had never been adopted and had come to The Hall when she reached the minimum age of twelve. She was a sweet, shy girl who sought approval from everyone. I tried to be nice to her once I knew her story.

The girls' stories came out in quiet moments or by happenstance. For most of them, their backgrounds weren't central to their lives anymore. Content with the present, they looked to the future. I wasn't ready yet to forget my past or share my story and no one pressed me. But Woodland Street grew more distant than I ever thought it would, and I realized that my childhood was better than some of these kids had experienced.

I even started to have some small amount of sympathy for the Hog River boys. I figured Bobby was probably in jail by now if he had kept on the same path. But some of the other boys who hadn't been so tough: Kevin, who had apologized to Lenore; the boy in the water who had first spoken out against what they were doing; the first boy to let go of my leg. I wondered what bad experiences had pulled them from their parents and landed them in the orphanage, and where they were now.

I missed Jacky but the summer days were busy with my kitchen duties, reading, Happy Lake, softball or croquet games on the large front lawn, and swimming in the pool over in the so-called bad-girls' yard. Sometimes I went to the movies with other kids, or we watched old movies on our own projector in the gym.

I wished The Hall had a basketball court, so I could play my favorite sport. One afternoon during a softball game, the nuns, Josefina, and Miss O'Brien sat under the shade of a huge maple tree watching the game, chatting among themselves.

I was playing first base, near where they were sitting, and approached them in between plays. "Mother, how come there's no basketball court here?"

"I don't know. Maybe no one has ever thought of it. Do you think the girls would use it if we had one?"

"I would."

"One isn't enough. Why don't you talk with the other girls, see if any of them would use it?"

At the end of that inning as the teams changed places, I called out, "Hey! How many of you would play basketball if we had a court?"

A bunch of hands shot into the air and several shouted responses—"Me!" "I would!"

I looked over at Mother, who smiled. "We'll put it on the list. But it'll be after the dining room and gym renovations. Maybe next summer or fall. Can you wait that long?"

A whole year from now? Would I even be here? I looked around me, at the building, the lush lawn, the girls, back at Mother.

"Yes, I can wait," I called back, feeling myself get awkward and happy at the same time, like something good had been settled inside me and outside too.

* * *

I had no roommate after Francie and liked having the room to myself. Toward the end of the summer, though, two sisters arrived and Mother asked me to give them the double room and take a smaller single room instead. The new room, painted white, was somewhat dark because it was long and narrow and had a fire escape right outside the window. It looked down on the nuns' garden from a different angle than the blue room. At night after curfew, I'd sometimes climb out the window and sit there by myself, absorbing the quiet and the different smells of nighttime. Sometimes I'd smoke, which was forbidden except in the gym and outside, and punishable by a week of restriction. I figured the fire escape counted as outside. I could have crept down the fire escape to the roof of a wooden passageway called "the tunnel" that connected all the buildings and from there lower myself onto the ground. It would be an easy walk to the street. But what would I be escaping from? Or to?

I went to the library every day. Mother urged me to read what she called the classics, books that all young people should read. I started with *The Adventures of Huckleberry Finn* because Mark Twain's home was around the corner on Farmington Avenue. I liked that book. I moved on to *Kim*, another orphan, and *Oliver Twist*, *Great Expectations*, and *Jane Eyre*. I began to wonder if all of the classics dealt with orphans, if Mother was trying to tell me something important, until I read *Little Women*, and *Wuthering Heights*, and the poems of Robert Frost.

Reading these books made me think about my parents. It surprised me to realize I didn't hate them anymore. I still didn't talk about them when the other girls shared their stories. It was from embarrassment mainly, but it didn't matter. They were dead and I was better off. But I couldn't tell people that. They would think I was crazy, or mean.

The library's tranquility absorbed me, and the books pulled me into different worlds. Engrossed in my reading, a messenger would be sent to tell me I was late for my kitchen job. And Josefina would shake her head and say I read too much for my own good. One day Mother was in the kitchen and heard her say that.

"Leave her alone, Josi. She reminds me of myself when I was her age," said the portly and aging nun. How odd, to think of her being young and like me.

CHAPTER 27

Growing Up

School started again. I was in the tenth grade. I celebrated my fifteenth birthday a bit late, waiting for Jacky to come home from boot camp. He looked handsome in his blue uniform. All the girls admired him. We talked nonstop every time I saw him. He went off again for more training before being assigned to a ship heading for the Mediterranean. He gave me twenty dollars in a beautiful card designed just for sisters and a framed picture of himself in his uniform, and promised to write often. My birthday came again as part of a celebration held at The Hall at the end of each month for all birthday girls, complete with cake and ice cream and a few small gifts.

Time went by quickly. Waiting for the basketball court to be built, still too young for an afterschool job except for the kitchen and trying to avoid Francie's fate, I used the study hour to do my homework. Honorable Mention came first. Soon I was a regular on the front blackboard where the teacher, Mr. Thomas, wrote in calligraphy with different colored chalks—first High Honors, usually one name; Honors with three or four names; and Honorable Mention with another three or four. The names stayed on the board all through that term.

Toward Christmas, Jacky's friend Ron called me asking to visit. He was in the Navy too but assigned in Bayonne, New Jersey, and came to Hartford a couple of weekends a month. He visited me at The Hall and started inviting me out. He was tall, around six foot four and well-built, not as slender as Jacky. His hair was short to meet Navy regulations but the top still curled and held its pale blond color. He had a gentle, sweet way about him, like a big lovable teddy bear. Mother approved of him, especially since our first dates included church attendance on Sundays. And he was always polite. In this way I started going back to Reverend Stevens' church and gradually became comfortable there. John and Judy greeted me with hugs.

Things were good all around: with Ron, at school, at home. I felt myself changing, I guess maturing and becoming more self-confident, although inside there was a big part of me that was the same girl I'd been when I climbed into the back of my father's car seeking safety.

I started hanging around with the older schoolgirls and some of the working girls who had already graduated from high school and moved to the second floor. Among the working girls, I saw that the ones who had quit high school had the hardest time getting good jobs. They held low-paying jobs such as clerks in small stores, and they frequently quit those jobs in frustration or were laid off. Mother was always trying to talk them into furthering their education. Two of them had started a beautician course and two more had enrolled in secretarial school. The high school graduates seemed happier with their jobs and where they might go in their companies. Working in an insurance company was the big thing in Hartford, the insurance capital of the world. I gave up my old idea of quitting school at sixteen. But somehow I couldn't see myself sitting at a desk in a big office in an insurance company.

Some of my new friends at The Hall didn't come from poverty as most of us did. One girl couldn't get along with her new stepfather. Another girl's mother had died, and her father, a rich businessman who traveled a lot, couldn't keep her at home. Another girl worked as a chemist in a pharmaceutical company but her wealthy Latin American parents wouldn't let her live alone in a strange city. They lived in Miami, Florida. The parents of these girls were all devout Catholics and had learned about The Hall through the church rather than through the juvenile or welfare authorities. I moved between this group of girls and those more like myself without difficulty. I was too young and maybe too unsophisticated to socialize with them, but I liked to talk with them. I especially liked the Latin American girl, Rosa, who played the piano in the gym like a professional and was smart and incredibly naïve at the same time. Socially she seemed younger than I. Once a man at work shocked her with some heavy necking on their first date. I told her men did that in the United States and she could say no. I had to get Jacky to explain it; she didn't believe me because I was younger. Perhaps I hadn't been too convincing because the memory of the Hog River had flashed through my mind as I spoke.

*   *   *

One icy cold Sunday afternoon, I received a phone call. I knew it couldn't be Ron because his ship had gone on a cruise.

"May, this is Stella."

"Stella Pagano?"

"Yeah. Did you hear the news about Alex?"

"What news?"

"He got killed in a car accident last night. The car hit a tree. Everyone else in the car was injured but he was the worst and died later in the hospital. My mother heard it on the news last night and it was in the paper this morning."

Alex and Chip, our summertime sweethearts. It seemed only the other day. I could hear Stella sniffling. Tears filled my own eyes. "How awful. He was such a sweet kid."

"I feel terrible about it. You know, he and Chip are at my school." She used the present tense, as if he were still alive.

"Yeah, I think I knew that. Thanks for calling to tell me, Stella. I miss you. How did you track me down here?"

"It took about ten phone calls. Doris Bergman finally told me where you were."

"Will you be at the funeral?"

"I'm not sure yet, but I hope so."

"How do you like Catholic school?"

"It's okay. I'm used to it now. Hey, I better go before my parents hear me talking. Maybe I'll get to see you at the funeral."

"Okay." I hung up. Miss O'Brien was watering the African violets on the window sill, and I slipped out of the room without having to explain my tears.

The next several days were filled with awful grief. I went to the wake, standing in a line stretching out of the funeral parlor and along the full

length of the block. It seemed like the whole high school had come. If
Stella was there, I didn't see her. I inched my way down the aisle to the coffin while the family sat to one side as Jacky and I had done at a different
funeral parlor. It shocked me to see Alex dead, his head shaven, his hands,
clean, pudgy, entwined with rosary beads, so unlike the dirty boy hands I
remembered. A sob broke from me and merged with the weeping of other
kids. Barely able to see through my tears I walked by each member of
Alex's large family quickly, mumbling, "I'm sorry...so sorry...I'm sorry,"
until I got out into the street again. Now I was sobbing hard, more than
the others. It was strange. On the bus home I realized I had included my
mother and father in my grief for Alex.

*   *   *

Ron came home most weekends. One weekend in early spring, we
went to the stock car races at Riverside Park just over the border in
Massachusetts. This particular night was a double-header and we lost track
of time. It was already ten-thirty when the program ended, curfew time.
We raced the twenty-five miles back to Hartford to find all of the lights
off at The Hall and the front door locked. I rang the doorbell. I could hear
it ringing but no one answered, no welcoming lights came on. I was locked
out. We sat on the front steps trying to decide what to do.

"Come home with me. My parents won't mind."

"I can't. I could end up in Long Lane. I told you what happened to
Francie."

"We can explain it all tomorrow. My mother can call."

"Let's check the windows."

We went around to the side of the building facing the apple orchard
and future basketball court. I saw a light on in a third-floor window.

"I think that's Mother's room." I tried to remember the sequence of
windows on the third floor but couldn't be sure.

We tried the ground-level windows into the basement and found the
ones to the kitchen and the storeroom next door all locked. The fourth one,
to a bathroom off the gym, was unlocked. I might have to sleep in the gym
if the nuns had locked the door to the first floor. But at least I was home.

I climbed through the window and let myself down onto a radiator.

Ron bent and kissed me. "I'll pick you up at ten-thirty tomorrow, okay? Wait at the window until you hear my car drive away."

"Don't go until I get inside."

"You'd better wait here till I'm gone. I don't want to be taken for a prowler if the cops drive by. Close the window when you hear my car leave."

He kissed me again and left. The caretaker and the cops occasionally walked or drove through the property at night. Ron was right to be cautious. When the sound of his motor reached me, I closed the window and let myself down to the floor, wondering how many kids knew about this open window and used it to ignore the curfew and hadn't told me about it!

The door to upstairs wasn't locked. I made my way to the schoolgirls floor walking in socked feet, shoes in hand. The wooden floor of the corridor creaked loudly. There was a transom window over Mother's door and the light was on. Would she emerge in her nightclothes, whatever nuns wore to bed? I quickened my pace down the darkened hallway to my own room.

The next day I waited for Mother to summon me about the curfew violation, which brought an automatic month of weekend restrictions. But she never mentioned it, so neither did I.

CHAPTER 28

Mother

One day, just before my afternoon shift in the kitchen, I was in my room writing a letter to Ron. I heard a commotion in the hall and went out to look. A new girl, Pam, and her roommate, Debby, flailed furiously at each other while several girls watched without trying to break it up. It got serious when Pam bit Debby's arm hard and held on. She drew blood. My stomach turned so violently that I thought I was going to throw up. My father's gangrenous arm, the smell of it, filled my head.

I told a younger girl, "Go get Mother. Quick!" The girl ran toward the stairs.

I knelt next to the two girls and pleaded with the biting girl to let go. "Come on, Pam, let go! You're going to get in trouble. You shouldn't bite people. It's dangerous. C'mon, let go!" I wanted to yank her by the hair to make her let go, but I was afraid it might make her bite harder. I imagined Pam lifting her head up with a chunk of flesh still in her mouth.

Out of the corner of my eye I saw Mother rushing toward us, robes billowing. She was not a young woman and her weight was substantial, but she flew toward us as if on wings. She stood over the two girls for a second or two, then without saying a word she swung her arm in a wide arc that ended with a hard uppercut punch to Pam's nose, which broke her grip on Debby's arm. Eyes as wide as quarters, Pam stared at the nun, who tugged Debby to her feet and walked her into the bathroom. What a solution!

"Human bites are the worst of all," she said. "Let's wash this off quickly."

Pam was restricted to her room for two weeks. In the dining room, she had to eat her food alone facing a corner. Debby went to the emergency room, and when she returned, she was restricted in the same way for starting the fight. Mother gave them a Monopoly game and a couple of books and warned them they would both be sent to Long Lane if they fought again.

The image of Mother punching Pam would remain in my memory for a long time. It was so unlike a nun. The more I thought about it the funnier it was. It wasn't at all like the punches at 416 Woodland.

*   *   *

Over the next weeks, it seemed that the relationship between Mother and me changed, the balance between us shifting a bit in my favor. Mother focused on me in a positive way, asking about my reading, complimenting me in front of the other girls for my grades or work around the place. She asked me to tutor a younger girl in reading. Sometimes she asked me to sit at the reception desk in the evening if I was hanging around in the gym. This meant I had to sign girls in and out and answer the phone. It was a position of trust and I liked doing it. And I pretty much followed the rules, giving no reason to be restricted or chastised.

One morning I woke up with a terrible sore throat, so swollen I could hardly swallow and when I did it was very painful. I decided to skip school and sleep in, hoping it would get better. But it got worse. In the afternoon I went down to the gym to buy a Coke, thinking the cold would help it. Each bubble bombarded the inflamed walls of my throat and I emptied the bottle out after only two sips. I went up to the TV room bathroom, which was brightly lit and had a large mirror over the sink, to look at my throat. I could hear Mother talking with Miss O'Brien in the reception room. I couldn't see much in the mirror and even opening my mouth was painful. Mother saw me as I was leaving the bathroom to go back to my room.

"What are you doing here? Why aren't you in school?"

"I have a terrible sore throat. I can hardly swallow." My voice was a whisper.

"Let me see." She backed me into the bathroom and stood me facing the window. "Open your mouth."

I did as she said, closing my eyes so I wouldn't have to watch her peering into my mouth. "Well, young lady, you're going to the doctor. Why didn't you tell me this earlier?"

"I thought it would go away." I surprised myself by starting to cry.

Mother patted my shoulder, it was almost a hug, and walked me into the reception room so she could telephone Dr. McDay's office. Then she called a taxi. I went up to dress and was ready by the time the taxi came.

Dr. McDay's office was just down the street a few blocks. He saw me immediately and looked into my throat for what seemed like a long time. "That's the worst sore throat I've ever seen. Your throat is almost closed. It must really be sore."

I nodded, trying not to swallow.

"Don't worry, I'll give you something for the pain and an antibiotic that will fix you up in no time. Tell Mother Superior to mash the pills in a spoonful of jam and let you suck it down, or tell her to make you a milkshake and take them that way." He chuckled and his Irish face seemed similar to Mother's in some way. "On second thought, I'll call her with these instructions."

Sure enough, when I got back to The Hall with the packet of pills, Mother took them from me.

"Dr. McDay said you won't be able to get these down unless we grind them up and put them in something smooth and tasty. I'll have Josie make you a little milkshake. Would you like that?"

I nodded, but didn't speak because it was so painful.

"Okay, now I want you to go up to your room and get in bed. Either Josie or I will be up with your milkshake medicine soon and after that you should try to sleep."

I moped my way upstairs already feeling better. Grown-ups who knew what they were doing were in charge. I didn't have to take care of myself.

*　　*　　*

Not too long after that Mother asked me if I wanted a nicer room. I accepted. This one was larger and brighter, with its own sink and a pleasing view out the south windows to the orchard, the new basketball court, and lawns. When I wanted to smoke I opened the window and leaned outside and Mother never caught me.

I loved that yellow room and there was no better one at The Hall. I would keep it. The bed had a green bedspread on it. Propped on the pillow was a huge white teddy bear Rob had won for me at Riverside Park.

Opposite the sink was a bureau. On top were photographs of Jacky in his uniform and of Rob and me smiling and hugging. At five foot eight and a half inches, I fit comfortably under his arm. My dimple shows in the picture and my short hair, laboriously curled overnight with wire curlers and sprayed stiff, looks nice, better than the old unruly ponytail. There was also a brown and white picture of Jacky and me as children. We're both serious, Jacky trying to hide his missing front teeth, me copying his example. It had been in the old album I had taken from our apartment, but now it had its own frame. So did one of my mother.

One day Mother had asked me about the photographs. Of course, she recognized Jacky and Ron and could tell that it was Jacky and me in the old photograph.

"Is that your mother?"

"Yes."

"She seems sad. Was she?"

I looked at the photograph, taken by the same distant relative, a professional photographer, who had taken the picture of Jacky and me. I wished he had also taken one of my father, but for some reason he hadn't. My mother had on a white dress with dark polka dots. I thought they were red, although I couldn't have been more than three years old when the pictures were taken. My mother's graying hair was pulled back and her face was almost unsmiling but not quite. There was the slightest hint of a smile if you looked hard enough.

"I guess she was. She had a lot of problems."

Mother nodded. "Sometimes life does that."

I often gazed at that picture and wondered how my mother had gotten so bad, how her life had gotten so off track. I recalled the explanations: the change of life, a broken heart over a dead baby, Dad's drinking. None of these convinced me. Mother Superior didn't seem to be having any change-of-life craziness. I decided it would be best either to remember my mother as she was in the picture, before things got bad, or to forget her. Keeping the photograph of her in the early years, looking at it every day, helped.

That room held everything I owned. It gave me what I needed. It was a place to sleep undisturbed, read, do my homework, be alone when I wanted to be.

One evening while writing a paper for a biology class, Mother came in after a quick knock. I had been smoking out the window earlier and was preoccupied with the possibility of lingering smoke. Mother didn't seem to notice it or the stack of empty Cokes I had piled next to my desk. I always forgot to take them back downstairs and return them to the machine. She looked over my shoulder to see what I was working on, reading the report I was writing about the human reproductive cycle. Without saying a word, she took the pen from my hand and changed the word "menistration" to "menstruation."

As she walked out, she said, "Please take these Coke bottles back downstairs where they belong."

I stared at the correction and plopped my head onto the blotter. This nun seemed to know everything.

A few nights later, after many warnings to follow the rule about returning empty Coke bottles back to the machine downstairs, I walked into my room late feeling mellow after a date with Ron. As the door swung open, it set off a domino effect of falling Coke bottles that had been arranged in a row starting just behind the door. Twenty of them skittered in all directions. The girls in neighboring rooms came running.

"What happened, you okay?"

"God, you woke me up!"

"Sorry. It's Mother trying to teach me a lesson."

The next day I put all the bottles in a laundry bag and carted them to the basement. Mother was standing in the kitchen doorway talking with Josefina. She watched in silence as I transferred each of the bottles from the bag to a crate next to the machine. A slight smile threatened to show through.

I laughed, tossed my head, and rolled my eyes. "You win."

CHAPTER 29

School and Work

At the end of my sophomore year, Mr. Thomas started to write the names on the honor roll. I watched, as if it were magic, as my name, Mary C. Kilgour, was moved from Honorable Mention to Honors. The entire classroom burst into cheers.

"Finally!"

"Congratulations!"

"Good work!"

Many of them were kids I'd known since kindergarten. Mr. Thomas stood in front of the room beaming at me and joined in the clapping. I grinned and blushed and liked it. I liked it!

I decided that I wanted to be called only Mary from then on. No more May. That was a kid's name from the past, a kid whose Scottish parents used to pronounce it Me. I wasn't that kid any more. At least, most of me wasn't. I couldn't wait to share my report card with Mother that night.

Every day wasn't perfect, of course. I sometimes—pretty often, actually—felt like an outsider, an observer of people with normal lives and families. I used to watch people on the bus to see how adults behaved, how they talked to each other, how men treated women and how women responded. I realized that nuns couldn't teach me everything. I watched the civilians who came to The Hall for communion breakfasts while I helped serve the food. Mother took to introducing me as "our scholar," or "our honor roll girl," beaming while I blushed.

The summer between my sophomore and junior years, some of us Hall girls got jobs on a tobacco farm in the countryside north of Hartford. We had to get up in the middle of the night to catch the bus that made a circuit of the city collecting the girls and women who sewed the tobacco leaves onto long sticks that would hang in the rafters of the sheds to dry. It was hard, hot work. Sticky brown tobacco juice went up my nose and stuck to the short blonde hairs on my arms. I knew I wouldn't want to do this kind of hard physical work for more than a summer, even though it wasn't as hard as the fieldwork Jacky had done. He used to come home covered in mud from dragging his butt along the rows of tobacco plants.

On my sixteenth birthday at the beginning of fall, I went job hunting. Within two weeks I was working in a supermarket, a new one in town, the Stop & Shop. I now had a new set of adults to observe, the men who managed the store and supervised my work and the full-time women who worked in the store's office and bakery departments. Teenagers hired with me came from Weaver and other high schools in the area and I became friends with several of them.

I liked the working world. The rules were clear and violators didn't last long: courtesy toward the customer, punctuality, accuracy and honesty in handling the cash register. I became one of the fastest cashiers and was always able to balance my cash at the end of my shift.

*   *   *

The thirty hours I worked each week dropped my grades from As to Bs by the end of the first semester. I was summoned once again to the dean's office, a new one this year named Lillian Leach, PhD. A thin woman with lots of wrinkles, she began talking as soon as I sat down, without a single pleasantry.

"Miss Kilgour, your teachers are worried about you. Your grades have dropped a lot since last year. They want to know what's going on." Her face was serious and she leaned forward across the desk waiting for me to respond.

This was an easy one. "I'm working now. I don't have as much time to study."

The dean's head jerked. "That's hardly an excuse, Miss. Your school work should always come before any afterschool job."

This surprised me. I had waited for a long time to turn sixteen so I could work. "I need the money. It's not as if I'm flunking."

Dr. Leach frowned. Her yellowed smokers' fingers tapped the desk. "Your teachers say you can do much better."

"Well, I could if I weren't working thirty hours a week. But I am."

"Your teachers are not sympathetic. School must come before work."

What was she talking about? Hadn't she read my file? "Well, I'm sorry they're not sympathetic. Frankly, it's really not their business."

The dean turned into a statue. She didn't move a muscle. But her eyes bored into mine.

"In other words, it's none of my business?"

"I didn't say that." I took a deep breath that turned into a sigh. "Your job is to discipline kids. But the teachers' job is to teach. My job is to learn as much as I can. And since I'm working, I only have time to learn up to the B level."

I thought my explanation would convince the dean. The opposite happened. It angered her and turned her face cherry red. She glared at me without speaking for a very long minute that made my whole body get back some of the wary tension it used to have.

"You are a rude and arrogant young lady. Go back to your class."

She didn't even give me a pass. I had to stop at the reception and get one from the secretary.

I got back to my English class in time to take part in a new round of the ongoing agony of reciting the soliloquy from *Macbeth* we were supposed to have memorized: "Out, out brief candle, life's but a shadow, a poor player who struts and frets his hour upon the stage," when the phone rang, summoning me again to the front office. This time it was the vice principal, Mr. Roseman, who had been at the school for years and had come to my father's funeral.

"May, what happened between you and Dr. Leach?"

"I go by Mary now, Mr. Roseman, not May."

"Okay. Mary. So tell me what happened."

I explained.

"Ah, I wish I'd handled this. I'd have known where you were coming from. She's not familiar with your background, being new. That's why she reacted so strongly."

I sensed a sympathetic ear. "Well, shouldn't she have read my file before calling me in?"

He propped his glasses on his forehead like my father used to do and rubbed his eyes with one finger from each hand. "Probably. Yes, she should have. Nevertheless, she's very annoyed and is insisting you be suspended. I've talked her down from two weeks to three days." A smile played across his face. "You were a little hard on her, Miss Mary. She wasn't impressed with your logic about differing roles."

"But I was being serious. I wasn't intentionally trying to be rude."

The vice principal explained what I needed to do to get back into school on the following Monday and dismissed me to go get my coat and leave the school. I went immediately to the supermarket and asked to work full-time during those three days.

When I told Mother that night what had happened, and that I would need an adult with me to get readmitted to school, she rolled her eyes and shook her head. "You'll have to track down a social worker to take you back to school. You know we don't venture out for such things."

The next day at one o'clock, while working a full eight-hour shift at the store, I saw Dr. Leach standing in line at a cash register down the row from mine. I'd never seen her shopping in this store before. Had Mr. Roseman sent her? To show her that I might be tempted to quit school to work full-time? I'd already given up on that idea but didn't intend to let Dr. Leach know that. She deserved to feel a little guilty, I thought.

After several phone calls, I found a social worker to escort me back to Weaver. I had to endure her official right to ask me all over again to explain myself and then listen to her advice for obeying adults and staying out of trouble. But I joked to Mother that she did get me back into school, even if she wasn't the governor.

Over time I learned how to balance work and school a little better. I made the honor roll most of the time, at least honorable mention, and accepted Ron's class ring. I asked everyone to call me Mary and most did, except for Jacky, who said when I remembered to call him Jack, he'd remember to call me Mary. It took a very long time for that to happen.

I started to hang around with a couple of girls from school I'd first met in seventh grade, but not from the shoplifting crowd, they didn't know about that. One of them, Margo MacDonald, had use of her parents' car and would pick me up for basketball games and other school social events. We'd go to Howard Johnson's afterward, the hangout of the "good kids." Sometimes Margo would hang out in the Hall gym with me and seemed comfortable doing so. She was funny and carefree and made me feel like a normal teenager.

*   *   *

During the summer between my junior and senior years, I worked full-time at the supermarket, learning the courtesy booth bookkeeping duties in addition to my cashier work, and got a nice raise.

At the beginning of senior year I got caught smoking in the girls' room. Mr. Roseman himself called me in.

"I haven't seen you since I rescued you from Dr. Leach last year. What happened?"

"Mrs. Bedford caught me smoking."

"Yes, she said she was surprised you didn't deny it. If you had denied it she couldn't have proven it and would have let you go."

"Really?"

"That's what she told me." He smiled. "Too late now. I'm giving you twenty hours of detention starting tomorrow."

My eyebrows went up. That was pretty stiff, just for smoking.

"Maybe you'll get some studying done. But, Mary, I'm not going to give you the demerits you would ordinarily get. You have too many on your record already from freshman and sophomore years. I don't want to jeopardize your college admission."

College admission? This was the first time anyone had assumed I would be going to college. Mother had focused her attention on grades and graduating but hadn't mentioned college. Had she? I tried to think back. That night I asked her what she thought about the idea of college.

"There's no doubt in my mind that you should go to college. You have the brains and it will open a lot of doors for you. It'll take discipline and commitment, of course. Do you think you have the discipline?"

"Maybe. I'll think about it."

CHAPTER 30

Off to See the World

I took the Scholastic Aptitude Test and scored high enough for acceptance to the University of Connecticut. I received a Weaver High School student scholarship, one for which kids earned the money by holding fundraising events and canvassing parents.

Jacky got out of the Navy on my high school graduation day. He traveled by train all day from Norfolk, Virginia. Halfway through the ceremony I saw him walk in and stand at the back of Bushnell Auditorium, scanning the stage for me. But we all looked alike in our green gowns and caps. I could see him but he couldn't tell me from the other girls. I wanted to shout, "Hey Jacky, it's me. I made it!"

Ron wouldn't be discharged until August, but he got liberty and came for my graduation. After the ceremony, Ron and I and Jacky and Rosa, the Latin American girl from The Hall, all went downtown to Honiss's for seafood. I hadn't been there for years. It was like Jacky and I had come full circle back to our mother's favorite restaurant, but we were traveling in a different orbit.

The next day, Jacky, Ron, and I went to pick up Jacky's graduation present: a black 1949 Pontiac. I was thrilled and a little bit scared to have my own car. But I'd need it to get to and from college. I'd decided to go to the Hartford branch of the university for the first year and continue living at The Hall. I wasn't convinced I'd like college, where I'd have to take it all seriously and go for the learning more than for the fooling around. I wasn't sure I had the discipline and commitment Mother said were necessary, let alone the brains she was so sure I had. But if I did, and I liked it, I'd transfer next year to the main campus thirty miles from the city, just beyond Times Farm Camp.

That summer I worked two jobs, full-time as a clerk-typist for the state employment service, which was an incredibly boring job, and part-time at the supermarket. No time for the lake, but I did swim in the evenings at the Marian Hall pool when I wasn't working at the supermarket. I always followed the same exercise regimen: one hundred laps of mixed strokes: the crawl, backstroke, crawl again, breaststroke, followed by the crawl, the sidestroke, and the whole sequence repeated. It took about fifty minutes and left me feeling fit and virtuous.

On Labor Day evening, when the sunset showed rippled blue clouds against a tangerine sky, I sat with Mother at a picnic table by the side of the pool after my swim. She had said her vespers prayers and was in the mood to talk.

"What will you major in?"

"Probably physical education. That's what I like best."

Mother shook her head. "You're too smart to spend your life bouncing balls."

"That's not all I'd be doing. I'd be teaching kids how to play sports. You influenced me by building the basketball court, you know." I had become The Hall's unofficial coach, taught the younger girls how to play in teams, and tried to organize games.

"Not intentionally. I did that to keep you here, to give you time to thrive." A mischievous grin lit her rosy face. "I think it worked."

I smiled. "I wasn't a complete angel. I did sneak in one night long after curfew and you never knew."

"I knew. I heard the bell and I heard you walking in the hall."

"Mother! Why didn't you let me in?"

"I wanted to test your resourcefulness and maturity. And I trusted Ron."

"You knew about the open window?"

"Of course. I opened it." The smile spread to her eyes, already squinting against the setting sun.

I wanted to hug her but knew the nuns disapproved of physical contact.

"I'm proud of you, Mary. You know that."

"Thank you, Mother." I felt my throat close up and looked away.

"What's Jacky up to now that he's out of the Navy?"

"He's working as a printer's apprentice. The pay's pretty good and so is the training he's getting, but he doesn't think he's going to stay there long. He's talking about reenlisting or maybe joining the Merchant Marines. By the way, I think I told you, he won't call me Mary until I call him Jack."

"Yes, you're both growing up. Well, whatever Jack does, I know he'll do well."

The pool was bordered by grass and rose bushes with flowers of many colors and shapes, large white and deep crimson, smaller pinkish ones and lovely ones of yellow and peach. It was peaceful and pretty.

"Guess what, Mother. You know Ron's about to be discharged from the Navy."

"Yes. What will he be doing?"

"He's going to work with his brother, in his contracting business."

"That sounds good."

"He's asked me to marry him."

"Yes?" She raised her thick silvery eyebrows. "And what did you say?"

I looked at the water and at the sun as it clung to the horizon of trees. "I said no. I'm not ready. I want to go to college and then out to see the world like he and Jacky did."

Mother nodded. "There's a lot of world out there. What will you seek in that world, dear?"

The question surprised me. Did I know? "Well, I think I want adventure, excitement." I stopped, waiting for a response. When there was none, I went on, "And I want to do good."

Mother looked at me intently, nodding her head, inviting me to say more.

"But I want tranquility too. Or serenity. Like here." I motioned with my arm toward the water and The Hall buildings behind me.

"Sounds like you want to become a nun, my dear."

I laughed. "I'm afraid not, Mother!"

She laughed.

I couldn't picture my future life very clearly. If I closed my eyes and thought real hard, I could see myself sitting in an easy chair under a good reading lamp in a pleasant living room. There were doors going off to other rooms, so it was an apartment or a house. There was music playing. The chair had flowers on it and there was a green rug on the floor. I was facing away, with my head down, reading, so I couldn't tell how old I was. But I was an adult, I was alone, it was very quiet, and I was content, resting after a busy day at work.

I didn't share any of this with Mother. We fell silent, comfortable with each other. The sky was turning dark and the stars were emerging one by one. The water lapped gently against the sides of the pool. The air was cool and smelled of roses. The laughter of the girls playing in the water sounded like wind chimes competing with birds. I looked at them swimming. They were younger, a new generation coming to The Hall. I hoped they'd find here what I had found.

E P I L O G U E

I did go to the University of Connecticut the next year and graduated in political science with honors in 1962. There was always the problem of what to do when the dormitory closed for the holidays. John and Judy Stevens, who had moved to a church in the southern part of the state, invited me to spend Christmas and Thanksgiving with them, and so did The Hall. Both places always made me feel welcome, but sometimes I chose to stay on campus and experienced the enormous solitude of a closed and nearly empty university.

For summers, I looked for jobs that came with living quarters. I worked in Maine as a waitress between my sophomore and junior years. The following summer I became an officer candidate in the U.S. Marine Corps, which gave me my first airplane ride and weekends in Washington, DC. The idea was to become a second lieutenant after I got my degree, but neither I nor the Marine Corps had any long-term obligation.

I was giving the Marine Corps serious thought, but the Peace Corps had been organized at the end of my junior year and I knew immediately that I wanted to volunteer. It was the adventure I had sought, along with the opportunity to do good. I applied and waited my whole senior year to get accepted.

My assignment as a teacher in a remote village in the Philippines truly was an adventure. At the time, my roommate, Ann, and I were not sure that we had accomplished very much. It took years, and a return to the Philippines, to learn that we had.

From the Peace Corps, I went back to the University of Connecticut, because I knew the political science department would find a way to help me pay for graduate school. Having earned only $54 a month for two years as a Peace Corps volunteer, there wasn't much money even to apply to other schools. Besides, Jack was an undergraduate at UConn by then, which was a big incentive for me to return. He finished his junior and senior years while I did a master's program part-time, working as a grad assistant to pay the bills. We lived in different apartments but had dinner together regularly, continuing our old habit of talking for hours.

Jack went on to Cornell to work on a master's, which later turned into a PhD in labor relations. He married a woman named Jan, who he met through me, had two children, and became a professor of business administration at a university in California. His wife was of Scottish descent too.

I went to Washington, DC, to work in the foreign aid program with the U.S. Agency for International Development and within a year was overseas on my first assignment as a foreign service officer. I had a long career with that agency, rising to the top of the career service by the time I retired twenty-nine short years later. In nineteen years of living and working in Pakistan, Colombia, Costa Rica, the Philippines, Liberia, and Bangladesh, I had plenty of adventures and also the opportunity to do good, just as I had dreamed of doing. A career helping poor countries and people seemed the ideal job. Social and economic development was an important, valuable, and difficult challenge that inspired me right to the day I retired.

Between my overseas postings, I worked at the headquarters in Washington, DC. During this time, I earned another master's degree and a PhD from Harvard University. My agency supported these studies, recognizing how complex international development is and how important continuing education is to finding solutions to problems that keep changing.

I never married, in part because the agency didn't allow women to continue working after marriage until 1972 and in part because I didn't fall in love with the men who fell in love with me, and vice versa. But I've had no regrets. That vision of me happily alone in a nice room reading and listening to music turned out to be true and, for me, the perfect fit.

After I retired, I started writing and volunteering in programs that deal with poverty and child neglect in the United States: Habitat for Humanity and the Guardian ad Litem program. I felt the circle to be unbroken.